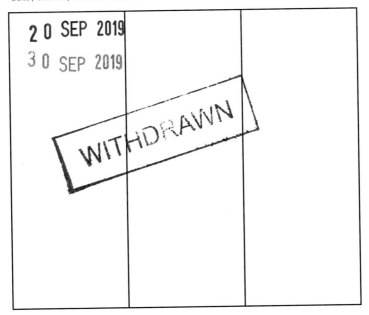

AND ON GUITAR ...

AND ON GUITAR ...

THE AUTOBIOGRAPHY OF
JIM CREGAN

WITH **ANDY MERRIMAN**

FOREWORD BY **SIR ROD STEWART**

First published 2019

The History Press
The Mill, Brimscombe Port
Stroud, Gloucestershire, GL5 2QG
www.thehistorypress.co.uk

British Library Cataloguing in Publication Data.
A catalogue record for this book is available from the British Library.

ISBN 978 0 7509 8566 6

Typesetting and origination by The History Press
Printed and bound in Great Britain by TJ International Ltd

Contents

Foreword by
Sir Rod Stewart

How can I possibly write a forward for such a backward thinking human being as Jim Cregan? I have friends in very high places, thankfully Jim is not one of them.

To be totally frank with you, I've always found this man to be somewhat tedious and boring. In fact, I always thought my used razor blades were dull till I met Jim Cregan. Tragically, he lacks any social graces and is devoid of any humour. To be honest, I've had better conversations with my kitchen table.

His sense of dress is not even up for discussion because it doesn't exist. He showed up at my wedding to Penny wearing a pair of bell-bottom trousers and high-heeled boots. The heel fell off one boot so he actually limped through the whole ceremony. It was so embarrassing, I could have killed him.

As far as his musicianship goes, the only word that comes to mind is 'rubbish'. It's totally lacking in style and depth and bereft of any soul and, worse still, Jim Cregan can't play football.

Together we've played our music to millions of people all over the world and stayed in more hotel rooms than the Gideon Bible. Touring can be tough and exhausting at times but if ever I felt rough before a show all I had to do was glance across the stage and see what Jim was wearing … and that would always make me roar with laughter.

As you have probably realised, this, so far, is all a wind-up, a ploy to get you to read J.C.'s book. The thing is, it's been said that if a man can count his true loyal friends on one hand he is truly blessed. Well, I'm blessed to have had Jim as a dear friend for over forty years.

Jim and I have written some wonderful songs together, including ASCAP-award winners 'Forever Young', 'Passion' and 'Tonight I'm Yours'. We've enjoyed fleeting debauchery, drunken falling down nights, hotel furniture rearranging, and general foolish behaviour as well as some deep, serious discussions about world affairs and relationships. Along the way, we've shared everything … but never our women (as far as I know).

We've created a million memories and had even more laughs, all of which are contained in this fantastic book.

A man could not have a better friend than you.

Love you mate …

Sir Rod

Acknowledgements

First of all, I'd like to thank everyone for their contributions, especially family members, who were, no doubt, partly hoping for something flattering to read about themselves. Good luck with that …

I'm eternally grateful to my kids, Camille, Mackenzie and Ava, for, well, everything.

To all the musicians I've worked with. Thanks for your dedication, skill and miscreant behaviour over the years. It's been a blast. As with any autobiography, there will be people upset because they're not in it and others annoyed because they are!

I must also state that in these 'riffing yarns' I have included many snippets of conversations that have taken place over the years, and that my memory may have played a few tricks. Some are verbatim, some are flights of fancy or even fictionalised. And while the anecdote about going on safari with Elton John is entirely true, my conversation with the water buffalo is slightly exaggerated.

I am grateful to all of the photographers whose work is reproduced. Some I have been unable to trace. Otherwise, unless credited, images are from my collection.

To all of the staff at The History Press, especially Mark Beynon and Alex Waite.

And finally my co-writer, Andy Merriman, without whom this whole farrago could have been avoided and my life would have been a lot easier.

1

High Kings, Ukuleles and Falcons

There was 'hot' music coming from behind the bar.

Captain W.E. Johns
Biggles in the Underworld

'Jim, you useless bastard, where are you?'

'Who's this? The line's a bit rubbish.'

'It's Mike, Mike Batt. Where are you?'

'I'm in LA, what's up?'

'I'm stuck and I need some help.'

'What have you done now?'

'I need you to go in the studio and stick a singer on a track I've recorded over here in London. There's a budget.'

'Of course,' I agreed, prompted by the promise of several beer vouchers for my trouble. 'And who's the artist?'

'Lemmy,' said he with a tone of voice I didn't recognise at first. It contained humour, for which he is renowned, but also a tiny bit of fear. Maybe he was thinking I might forgo the vouchers and just stay home and scratch my bum. 'It's a track called the "Eve of Destruction" and it's part of an album I'm doing on songs from that period with the London Philharmonic Orchestra, so there ... Barry McGuire, you know the one?'

'Yes, I know it,' I replied, not exactly thrilled with the prospect, and fighting back a tsunami of indifference. 'What exactly would you like me to do?' I asked, dreading the reply.

'Just nip in to Ocean Way Studios, stick the vocal on the back track I've recorded and return it to me. I'll mix it and take it from there. Piece of cake.'

'OK, I can do that.'

'You'll need to bring the track to Lemmy, so he can rehearse. He doesn't drive so he won't pick it up.'

'OK, I can do that.'

I should point out here that Mike's taste is very conservative and exceptionally musical. He's classically trained and regularly conducts symphony orchestras. He discovered Katie Melua and has a stack of platinum records even though I've played on many of them.

So, armed with a cassette, I went to Lemmy's apartment, which was located within walking distance of the infamous Rainbow Bar and Grill on Sunset Boulevard. Renowned for its groupies and pizza, it has played host to almost every touring band that there ever was. Back in the day I was there, rubbing shoulders with Joni Mitchell and Elton John while Led Zep monopolised all the best-looking women. Bastards. Later it was eclipsed by other bars, but still remains an old favourite and there's usually some recognisable face in there.

Lemmy's home was a one-bedroom flat in a very ordinary block quite like a motel with a walkway all around the second floor giving a view of the unnamed-contagion-ridden pool. I knocked and waited at his door. There were some strange noises.

Slowly the door cracked open and a girl slipped through the gap, all black vinyl miniskirt and smudged mascara. There were no formal introductions.

'Hello,' I said to the shadowy figure inside the darkened hallway. 'I'm Jim. Mike Batt sent me to give you this tape.'

'Come in,' he said opening the door wide, revealing himself for the first time. 'I'm Lemmy.'

And there he was, stark naked, except for a droopy pair of greyish paisley briefs. His pale, white, luminescent torso in vivid contrast to the multiple tattoos that covered his arms. Complete with cigarette and that shit-kicking grin.

'Wanna beer?' he asked, ushering me in.

'Sure,' I said, wondering if he would get dressed any time soon.

Now, I've done a lot of travelling, seen many unusual sights and consider myself somewhat unshockable.

Rubbish.

Lemmy's flat was crammed with an enormous collection of Nazi memorabilia. There was a mannequin in one dark corner dressed in a Gestapo SS uniform which scared the living daylights out of me. A Luger automatic pistol and a Nazi dagger graced the coffee table amongst the beer cans and overflowing ashtrays. Swastika flags, helmets, guns and uniforms were everywhere you looked. He even had one of those banners they used to hang from balconies after they had taken over the Ritz in Paris.

I was completely shocked.

Unlike his surrounding paraphernalia, Lemmy was, however, very friendly and thankfully took great pains to tell me he definitely wasn't a Nazi or a Fascist; he just liked collecting this stuff. I was much relieved. Then, still in his underpants, he showed me an old magazine featuring him on the front cover, cranked up the ghetto blaster with his latest album on it and played his Rickenbacker bass along with it, giving me a free concert.

I have to admit there was something very likable about him.

We drank our warm beer and eventually I escaped back out into the sunny LA afternoon.

'See you Wednesday,' I called back to him. 'Maybe with some trousers?'

I duly picked him up for the session and was happy he was wearing his trademark black everything, complete with that hat.

'Can you just pull over here?' he asked after a couple of minutes.

'Sure,' I replied.

Then I notice we are outside a liquor store and he soon emerges with a bottle of any old whisky. It's 1.30 in the afternoon and I'm worried …

So, we arrive at Ocean Way Studios in Hollywood and greet the engineer and assistant who are both friendly and courteous. We sit and chat for a while in the control room looking out through the glass to the main recording room. The mic and headphones are waiting for our artist and there's a semi-circle of 8ft-high acoustic screens behind the mic, which is an absolutely normal set-up.

'I can't sing out there like that,' announces Lemmy.

'Like what?'

'Like that, with you all watching.'

'What do mean, watching?'

'Y'know, staring at me while I'm singin'.'

'We won't be staring at you, we'll be listening.'

'I'm not doin' it.'

This goes on for a while until we agree to put a full circle of screens round the mic and turn down the lights. Lemmy disappears into this grey void. A feeling of dread seeps into the air-conditioned room. We ask him to run through the song, so we can get some levels.

The disembodied voice grunts, 'Hmm.'

We run the track and in a moment of premonition, I ask the engineer to record everything. The banter in the control room has escalated and we are now supposing that maybe Lemmy can only sing naked. Or he's snuck somebody into the studio to help him … er … relax … or … the imagination takes wings. Which is more than can be said for the vocal performance. It's terrible.

'OK Lemmy, we need to do it a couple of times now we've got the levels,' I lied.

'No that's it. I won't get it any better.'

'But that was just the run-through.'

'You took it though, didn't you?'

'Yeah … but …'

'Well, we're done then.'

DEAR GOD IN HEAVEN.

I've got nothing. Nada. Zip.

'Please, Lemmy,' I beg. 'Just one more take.'

'No man, sorry that's it.'

So, using every bit of Irish persuasion taught by generations of Paddys down the years, I gave him the full blarney. Both barrels for about fifteen minutes. Not a chance. Nowhere. Complete failure. Batt had paid in the region of $8,000 … to get nothing.

'Can you give me a lift?' he inquires, all whisky and pallor.

'Yes, of course.'

We climb into my black 560 SEL and rip out of the parking lot.

'Could you drop me round the corner?'

'You don't want to go home?'

'Naah … take me to the strip club.'

So, we said our goodbyes on the corner of Sunset and La Brea outside a very grimy club and that was the last I ever saw of him. Living the Dream. Telling Mike Batt about it was not my favourite moment but it had an interesting postscript.

Lemmy was about to tour the UK so Mike arranged to re-record the vocal in London, producing it himself. I warned him, but to no avail. And exactly the same thing happened! Maybe Lemmy had heard Frank Sinatra supposedly only did one take. Anyway, through the magic of computers it turned out somewhat bearable.

Dear Lemmy. The real thing.

RIP.

★★★

In an extraordinary and coincidental twist of fate, just a couple of hundred miles away and merely a few months after Lemmy's birth, I was born, at an early age, to Irish parents, Robert and Evelyn Cregan, in Yeovil in 1946 (hence earning Rod Stewart's moniker as 'the Somerset Segovia'). Third in the trio of offspring, Maurice and Joyce had already made their debuts in the Cregan band before I appeared. I never knew any of my grandparents, but that won't stop me mentioning them. My maternal grandmother was a headmistress in the town of Falcarragh (County Donegal) where my grandfather was the postmaster. My paternal grandparents, the Cregans, were staying in Scotland at the time my dad was born. Grandfather was a stud groom working for the Ponsonby family who had estates in Scotland and Ireland. He was in charge of the stables and responsible for the horses which pulled the carriages. My dad was put up on a horse when he was 2 and promptly fell off. He never got on a horse again.

The family later moved to Limerick, and Dad, one of three siblings, attended the 'Christian Brothers' school that was described in Frank McCourt's book *Angela's Ashes*. He left there at the age of 13. He met my mother, Evelyn Finola Boyle, in Dublin and then both travelled to England in search of work.

Dad had a variety of jobs. He worked as a blacksmith and as a rep for the National Cash Register Co. During the war, he worked in a factory, putting tails on Hurricane fighter planes, then as a postman and aircraft fitter at Westlands before being gainfully employed in a company that manufactured refrigerated display units. He was also, and let's keep this between us ... a smuggler. Not of the kind that fought with dragoons and customs men in Cornish coves. No, his job was to smuggle suitcases full of Irish Hospital Sweepstake tickets to Kilburn where they would be sold. It was legal to own the tickets in the UK, but against the law to sell them or bring them over. It was his way of helping the poor, so I like to think of him as a sort of Robin Hood type, although he looked like a gangster. So, in fact, he was more George Raft than Errol Flynn. He was self-educated: his learning came from the radio and books, but he refused to rent a television set until I had finished my O-levels. 'And put that guitar away,' was a constant refrain ...

My mum was one of five siblings and worked as a hairdresser in Dublin until she married Dad and they moved to London. She eventually became a full-time housewife, looking after the three of us. I was a chronic asthmatic and spent a lot of time off school. When I was 5, it was thought that the sea air might improve my condition and we all uprooted to Parkstone, near Poole in Dorset, where Dad got a job as a travelling salesman.

This was a great and generous gesture on Dad's behalf, but sadly it made no difference to my health. What the asthma really needed was a massive dose of testosterone and so by 15 or so, I was pretty well over it. I'm not sure that my brother Maurice or my sister Joyce, then aged 13 and 11, were that enamoured with me for instigating the move. Fortunately, they aren't the types to hold a grudge for something that happened in 1951 and so both forgave me last year.

The move did, however, begin a love affair with the sea, which continues to this day. I was in the 1st Lilliput Sea Scouts at the age of 11 and I was taught to sail in a fixed keel boat by one of the seniors. He got me out on Whitecliff Bay, tied off the jib, then settled himself in the bottom of the boat and said, 'Right, I'm going to have a sleep. Don't wake me unless we hit something – and don't bloody hit anything!' And that was it. No health and safety; I had to learn to sail.

Ours was a working-class family with aspirations to be successful. The family struggled to make ends meet, but never went hungry. We were taught good manners and to treat everyone equally. I feel comfortable with anyone from any background. This philosophy has formed my intense dislike of injustice and authoritarian regimes, which has stayed with me all my life. One of my heroes is Nelson Mandela. Any man who is locked up for twenty-six years by a vile racist government and, on release, forgives them and embarks on a programme of reconciliation, is a man I choose to admire.

Mine was a happy childhood, growing up in the 1950s in the south of England. I used to read a lot and my heroes were the flying ace, Biggles, and schoolboy William Brown, Richmal Crompton's eponymous hero of the *Just William* books. Of course, I wanted to be one of them, but I suppose it was no coincidence that both these fictional characters had friends called 'Ginger' (their real names were never divulged) and as I sported a shock of fiery red hair, I was reduced to playing the role of supporting character rather than the lead. I was even called Ginger when I was at Longfleet Infants school in Poole. When I later attended Poole Grammar School, I joined the school boxing team, so people tended to leave me alone. Luckily, they never found out that I wasn't much good.

There was the occasional use of the slipper by my dad if it was deemed necessary, but in terms of discipline, our mother was more pushy about exams and qualifications. Poor Joyce was sent to a convent school, which she hated because of the bullying nuns. She is seven years older than me and used to look after me when I was a toddler. My brother Maurice and I never got on as kids. He still describes me as 'a spoiled brat', which, of course, I am. But as soon as I turned 18, and could buy a round of drinks, we started a friendship which gets closer with each passing year.

Dad always had a car, which was unusual in those days; a Ford V8 and he used to arrange mystery tours on a Sunday afternoon. It wasn't much of a mystery as we usually went to Lyme Regis or Weymouth. And our picnics in those days weren't exactly lavish – it was soon after the war and so there was still rationing, but I recall those days with great fondness.

My Uncle Ernie, my dad's brother, who incidentally looked more like my dad than my dad, always used to recount that our family were descendants of Brian Boru, the greatest of the Irish high kings, famed in saga, legend and public houses. I was once in a pub with my then wife, the singer Linda Lewis, who proudly announced to the Irish landlord, 'My husband is a descendant of Brian Boru.' Generously he gave us endless free drinks. 'This royalty business is great,' I thought but it was all fantasy, of course, and later my dad sadly had to explain it was all blarney, invented by Ernie.

We had lots of relatives across the Irish Sea and I remember gifts of turkeys and butter sent by an uncle, while we were still under the administration of rationing. I visited the family in Ireland a couple of times – once when I was 12 and more than a decade later. We visited Ballybrittas, County Laois, which I was sure was the village where my Auntie Sally lived. By now I was 22 and went into a shop and asked if Sally O'Donnell still lived nearby and the shopkeeper's response was, 'No, she's moved away, but you wouldn't be that little Jimmy Cregan, would you? Nice to see you again.' I hadn't been there for ten years or more and now had long hair and a beard. Must be pretty quiet round here I thought – either that or the shopkeeper has a photographic memory.

Playing music has dominated my life since I was 9, when a friend of Age's gave me a ukulele. Oh, I'd better explain that 'Age' is my dad. My brother Maurice nicknamed him 'Age' – for no apparent reason. Oh, and we call Mum 'Plum' – again the Cregan archives offer no explanation. Anyway, I was given this ukulele, which, believe it or not, only had one string, so I couldn't play chords, but I could pick out melodies and by the time I had learned Bill Haley's legendary tune 'Rock Around the Clock' a few months later, I was totally immersed in music – to the extent that Age would lock the ukulele in the cupboard and not let me have it until he had checked to make sure I had done my homework properly.

When I was 12, as a Christmas present and a reward (not sure whether it was for my ukulele playing or my homework) my parents gave me a guitar and I guess that I haven't really put the instrument down since. My first public performance was given at Poole's 'Central' (there was only one) library singing Irish rebel songs and I'm convinced I have been under MI5 surveillance ever since.

Now, I remember that our family were staunch Irish Republicans. When Bobby Sands, a member of the Provisional IRA, died in 1981 after sixty-six days on hunger strike at the Maze Prison, there was much political discussion in the house. Dad stated that he admired that Sands starved himself to death for his principles. 'Very few people would do that,' he declared. I remember singing Republican songs at home that I had learned from family members. Our house was culturally Irish and our influences were Gaelic.

Listen to my sister and brother on the subject. Firstly, Joyce, 'I don't remember that at all. You're wrong.' And my brother, 'Nonsense, where did you get that from? Complete rubbish!'

Now, this is an important stage of the book, because, dear reader, you must decide how much of a reliable narrator I really am. Because if you call into question my memory and my anecdotal material, then we are in trouble. So, I suggest you stick with my stories throughout and certainly at this stage – because I'm not going to tell you where Maurice and Joyce live in case you do try and verify these adolescent memories.

At home, my dad really did sing 'When Irish Eyes are Smiling' and 'Phil the Fluter's Ball', but it was my brother, Maurice, who was initially influential in my musical education. He liked Sinatra and Ella Fitzgerald and came home one day with a jazz album by André Previn and Shelly Manne playing *My Fair Lady*. The sleeve notes said they had no rehearsal and had never worked together before. The passages of improvisation blew me away. We also had Shubert's *Unfinished Symphony*. All right, I don't think there was much vamping going on there, but it shows that I was being influenced in quite different directions, but that seemed normal ... and still does.

Our family weren't particularly religious, but the Catholic Church was a way of life back in the old country. The local Catholic primary school was pretty awful with so few kids passing the eleven-plus exam, so Mum decided to send me to the Protestant school in the hope of a better education. This was such sacrilege that the old Catholic priest refused to confirm me into the faith, so I didn't have first communion or any of the other rituals. Mum despised his petty mindedness. Eventually Maurice and I, dressed in our Sunday best, would leave the house for eleven o'clock Mass but then go fishing down at Poole Quay.

Strangely enough it was my experiences on acid some years later that brought me back to believing in a higher power …

I was lying on my bed in a house in Fulham tripping madly and staring at a crack in the ceiling running from left to right. Ever so slowly the crack appeared to open like a giant pair of lips and this incredibly bright white light began to pour out. It should have been blinding but it wasn't. The lips parted and the whole ceiling disappeared, filling the room in the dazzling display. An enormous sense of peace and love flooded through me and time stood still. It was as if I had caught a glimpse of heaven. In that moment I believed I understood everything and the meaning of life, love and the cosmos. It was a profound moment of clarity and later I read that I may have experienced the White Light described in *The Tibetan Book of the Dead*.

Since then I have had a very open mind to the possibilities of forces unknown to us existing in a parallel universe. I later chose to follow the teachings of Christ although I am not religious in the traditional sense and don't attend church. In fact, I have a healthy disrespect for the Catholic Church and many of the organised religions. My parents must have felt the same because they refused to send me to the local poorly performing Catholic secondary school.

So off I went to Poole Grammar, where, at the age of 14, I formed my first band, called the Falcons. We were an instrumental group – a sort of Wessex version of the Shadows. One of my heroes was Hank Marvin. The Falcons consisted of schoolfriends; Mike Domay, Barry, who died tragically in a motorcycle accident at the age of 16 and drummer Bill Nimms, who was my best friend at the time. He became a very good artist and graphic designer.

We began playing in youth clubs and then gigs around Poole. 'Sidetrack' was the first song I wrote, only ever unleashed to an unsuspecting public on one occasion, which was at a school concert.

I borrowed an electric guitar for our first gig, which was held at the local youth club in Church Street, Lower Parkstone. It was pretty scary, although enjoyable. My main aim was to try and impress girls in the audience. I've been attempting to do that with varying success ever since. We put a Shadows cover band together and played there as often as they would put up with us.

The Falcons continued to perform until halfway through the first year of my A-levels, studying art, English literature and geography at Poole Grammar School where I had somehow managed to achieve five O-levels when my dad got a job in London and the family upped sticks and whatever else we used for cutlery. I really didn't want to move as all my mates were in Poole – not to mention the band – and I just wanted to carry on at school.

I also had my first serious girlfriend and wanted to be with her, although a recently discovered photograph of her holding my guitar in a plastic bag and looking bored probably didn't bode well for the future of our relationship. However, I didn't 'kick off'. I just accepted that there was nothing I could do about the move and accepted my lot with what I think was remarkable stoicism.

My sister Joyce was married by now and brother Maurice was in the army, so it was just me living in the suburb of Eastcote with my parents and although I wasn't happy about leaving my friends and the band, looking back, if I hadn't moved to London, I might not have had the career that I have had.

I enrolled at the Harrow School of Art and then also at Harrow Technical College to continue with my English lit A-level. The education system held no interest for me; I spent the next two years pretending to get an education. On the more than odd occasion that I was 'AWOL', I used to tell staff at the art school that I was at the technical college and vice versa. The two places of 'learning' never seemed to check up with each other and I was mostly in the clear. I learned a lot at art college – particularly at the life class which featured a beautiful nude model. It was the first time I had seen a naked woman. I was transfixed and only disturbed from this reverie when the teacher barked, 'Put pencil to the paper, boy. Stop gawking and start drawing.'

I've remained very close to my siblings and we now live near each other in Dorset. All the family have always been really supportive about my career choice. When Joyce was older, I was in a band called Blossom Toes. We would finish an all-nighter then drive to Dorset and park our blue van outside her house, sleeping till late in the morning when she would feed us all porridge.

Both Joyce and Maurice visited me at various times when I was on tour with Rod, as did my mum and dad. In June 1979, sitting around in a hotel bar, Rod and I were reminiscing about our families, especially our brothers. As we were due in New York for about a week, whilst playing Madison Square Garden, we thought we would invite our dads and brothers for a few days' holiday. The plan was realised and shortly after, my brother Maurice, Rod's brothers Donny and Bobby, together with our fathers (both coincidentally called Bob) were ensconced in our hotel. There were helicopter rides over the city, which were great fun except for the fact that Rod's father had neglected to close his door properly and almost fell out.

Meanwhile Maurice and I began to feel a little guilty that our mother had been left out, and so we schemed to bring her to New York as a surprise for Dad. Enter Federico Gastaldi. Now Federico happens to be the best socially connected man I have ever met. Equally at home with musicians, sportsmen, socialites and royalty, he now works for Formula 1. For some reason he wanted to be adopted into the Cregan clan – so he took it upon himself to oversee entertainment for my family.

Back in those days it was possible for a married couple to share a passport with both names and photos. I know, it sounds bizarre but that's how it was. Now, this presented a problem as my father had locked the passport in the hotel safe. There was no way Mum could get to New York without it.

So Maurice, masquerading as my dad, volunteered to try and get the passport back. Using his delusional 'smooth talking bastard' skills but simply just lying through his teeth, he approached the front desk manager. Somehow, we knew that sending a passport across international borders without the owner, was highly illegal. Maurice was understandably nervous.

'Good afternoon, sir,' he oozed, flashing his perfect smile. 'May I have my passport please? It's in the hotel safe.'

'Certainly sir, may I have your name?'

And my smooth-talking brother replied, 'Maurice Cregan.'

Ooops.

After searching fruitlessly through a large pile, the manager apologised but no such passport was in the safe.

Oh bollocks.

Slightly red-faced, Maurice returned to the gang in the bar and confessed that he had failed. It was agreed that a new plan would have to be hatched and pretty quickly if we were going to get our mother over before it was time to go back. 'Let's tell Dad we need to buy some jewellery, to bring back to Mother, to make up for her having to stay home,' I said.

So, we ran upstairs and burst into Dad's room, armed with the new scheme.

'Hey Dad, Maurice and I have seen some earrings in the jewellers in the hotel lobby. They would be a perfect gift and with your passport you can get them tax-free. All you need to do is get the passport from the safe and leave the rest to us.'

'Not bloody likely,' says yer man. 'You lot would pay retail and if I'm going to get a present, I'm going to get it myself at my New York discount.' Father had never been here before, but that wasn't going to stop him. You see, sometime previously, in England, I had seen a very beautiful second-hand Mercedes 450 SEL and wanted to buy it. I asked father if he would negotiate it for me.

'No, you should be able to take care of that,' he says, toasting his aged feet in front of the fire.

'Well, if you don't help me, I'll pay the asking price.'

In seconds, he was fully dressed. Coat, hat, gloves, glasses and clean underwear. Arriving at the used car lot in Sandbanks, later to become one of the most expensive used car lots in the world, he went into action. The salesman followed Dad around the car as he kicked the tyres, grumbling and muttering under his breath.

'I don't think much of this,' he said, pointing to an imaginary dent.

By now, I was so embarrassed that I hid around the corner, not wanting to see the carnage that followed when Dad went to work on this poor unsuspecting guy.

About twenty minutes later Dad emerged with a grim look on his face. 'He wanted too much money. He started off at £11,000 and I could only get him down to £7,300.'

'What! You didn't take it?'

'Of course I did. I'm not bloody stupid! Melvin also offered me a job as chief negotiator.'

'You're on first name terms with this guy already?'

'Sure. We're old pals and as soon as the wounds to his wallet have healed, we're going for a beer.'

Now you can understand what I was up against. But I digress. Maurice came up with the new wheeze and approached the front desk again.

'Dad's had an accident. The A&E department needs some iden-tification and all he's got is his membership card to "Geriatrics Anonymous" and they say that's not enough. So please may I have his passport, so he can get treatment?'

'I'm not sure about this sir, it's most irregular. No, I'm afraid in this instance, I can't help, but if there is anything else …'

Raising himself up to his full 5ft 10 and a half, Maurice, in his best retired British Army officer's voice, barked, 'My name is Captain

Maurice Cregan, and this is my father we're talking about. If you know what's good for you, you'll get the document immediately or suffer the consequences.'

Feeling like an extra in *The Bridge over the River Kwai* the desk clerk slouched off, giving Maurice a look like a sharpened bayonet and meekly handed over the passport. Success at last!

Later during our stay, the desk clerk saw Dad crossing the lobby with Maurice. Beckoning my brother over, he asked how come Dad was up and about.

'Miraculous cure,' Maurice grinned. 'Must be the Manhattan air.'

It then fell to Federico to get the passport back to my mother in time for her to come to New York. Of course, he knew someone at British Airways and somehow persuaded a pilot to carry the passport back to Heathrow. We then called Mother and threw her into panic by insisting she board a plane the next day. Mum would normally require seven days to get her hair done and buy a new nighty.

Now for the fun part. Federico told Dad that he had this beautiful Argentinian lady friend in her 50s arriving the next day. She was well versed in the arts of love and Federico thought, as it was a boys' weekend in New York, Dad might like to meet her, so to speak. The old man was very flustered.

'Freddie! I couldn't possibly entertain the thought.'

'No of course,' Maurice and I chimed, loyal sons to the end, 'but who is she, Freddie, and what's she like?'

'Her father was a diplomat, like mine, but she was too wild for the family and branched out on her own, starting the most exclusive escort agency in Buenos Aires.'

'And what does she look like?' we asked.

'Just amazing, petite, slender with long wavy red hair, a sort of Rita Hayworth type.'

Freddie had obviously done his homework, as Miss Hayworth was one of Dad's favourite film stars.

'Well, maybe I could just meet her,' Dad offered nervously. So, the next evening we order a limousine to take us to Kennedy Airport. 'I'm not sure about this,' said father, straightening his tie, tousling his hair, and checking his nose for drips.

'Oh, come on Dad, where's the harm in this? You're just going to say hello and that will be that. Oh, by the way, it's quite a coincidence, but she's staying in our hotel. I think it's room 5130.'

'Jesus, Mary and Joseph, that's next door to me, I'm in 5132.'

'What are the chances of that, I wonder,' murmured Maurice.

Despite the air conditioning, Father is beginning to perspire heavily. Before long, we pull up outside the airport. Freddie tells us to wait in the car while he goes to collect Dad's date. The tension in the car was building rapidly, Father was fidgeting and wiping his brow. Federico is about 6ft 4 and we could see his head above the rest of the crowd but couldn't make out who he was with.

Suddenly it was clear who was crossing the sidewalk. Dad's eyes popped out like a rude child's tongue, his shocked face resembling Munch's painting *The Scream*. Uncharacteristically agile, he threw himself to the floor of the limo shouting, 'Bloody Hell, what's she doing here?' Maurice and I collapsed with laughter as our mother opened the door.

'Well, this is nice,' she smiled. 'Bob, what are you doing on the floor?'

'I dropped my glasses.'

Mum never knew and we never said …

2

What's Our Time, Mr Wolf?

You take up an instrument, and you have a friend for life.

Stanley Lane
(Ronnie Lane's dad)

So, following my migration to the smoke, the Falcons had flown away and despite developing a love of drawing and design, music still dominated my life. With new-found friends in West London, we formed a new group, the Coronado Four, named after the Coronado – a kind of somewhat lacklustre Fender guitar. The band consisted of yours truly (lead guitar and vocals), Adrian Sumption (rhythm guitar and vocals), the bass player was Ken McKay, who was in Johnny Kidd and the Pirates, and drummer Pete Hocking completed the quartet.

Although I was the only one of the group studying art, it was quite extraordinary how many bands in the early 1960s had met at art college. Jeff Beck attended Wimbledon School of Art, Eric Clapton was at Kingston Art College and, of course, the most iconic band with this background was the Rolling Stones. Charlie Gillett, author of the rock and roll anthology *The Sound of the City*, wrote:

> An increasing number of school-leavers looked for ways to delay the decision of what job to take, and many opted for art school courses in printing, graphics, commercial design, and photography – as well as traditional painting and sculpture courses. Kids found kindred spirits at art colleges who shared a devotion for Ray Charles, Howlin' Wolf and ad-hoc bands formed out of casual jam sessions.

And this was very true of my experience. I had moved on from listening to Little Richard and Elvis and had discovered the records of Jimmy Reed, Sonny Boy Williamson, Howlin' Wolf, and B.B. King. The Coronado Four started by covering Beatles songs, but then wanted to play more blues. We also weren't keen on the name of the band and because of our new direction, we morphed into the Dissatisfied Blues Band. We were managed by Chris Morrison who went on to handle Blur and the Gorillaz, amongst others. He was studying with me at Harrow Tech and had seen the band. But he still wanted to manage us anyway.

We initially played loads of local pubs and youth clubs. A review in the *Ruislip and Northwood Gazette* from June 1964 stated, 'The group described the reception they received at the Hesdin Youth Club on Saturday night as "the best ever." Within an hour the hall had its full quota of 300 teenagers and many others were turned away.'

Fortunately, those unlucky punters had the opportunity to catch us at more prestigious venues in the months to come when we found ourselves supporting some big-name acts at the famous Marquee Club in Soho's Wardour Street. The London scene was pretty vibrant in those days with lots of clubs that have mainly disappeared. All that remains of the Marquee, which closed in 1988, is a Blue Plaque which states, 'Keith Moon played here'.

Opening for the Spencer Davis Group, I seem to recall that Stevie Winwood was still at school and he turned up for the gig in his short trousers. Having checked this out, he must have actually been about 16 – so either he was a slow developer or I'm getting confused with William Brown (although he was never in any of our bands). We also fronted for the Kinks and the Yardbirds and got to know them quite well. We played with them at a blues festival in Uxbridge and Eric Clapton came up to us at the end of our set and congratulated us. At that stage we had no idea that these bands would become so legendary – they were just Ray's or Eric's band. It was an incredible scene and we probably took it for granted, not realising how unique this was.

There was quite an established rhythm 'n' blues and jazz venue in a room above the Railway Hotel in West Hampstead. It became the haunt of a number of well-known musicians. The club was Klook's Kleek, which was named after an album, *Klook's Clique*, by the jazz drummer, Kenny Clarke, whose nickname was 'Klook' – originally 'klook-mop' – an onomatopoeic nickname due to the unexpected 'bombs' he would drop behind the soloist. I had been there on many an occasion, seeing people like the Cyril Davies All-Stars, Zoot Money and the Graham Bond Organisation. One appearance at the club became legendary – John Mayall was topping the bill and Jimi Hendrix dropped by to jam with the band ...

Promoters started bringing over American blues artists for concert and club tours and by the mid-1960s John Lee Hooker, T-Bone Walker and Champion Jack Dupree had all appeared in the UK. Howlin' Wolf was one of the Delta blues stars who we worshipped. In fact, our signature piece, 'Smokestack Lightning', was one of his more celebrated songs. Charlie Gillett described him beautifully as providing 'a frightening menace to his records even when he was trying to be friendly – a mournful vocal which sounded as if he might swallow the microphone and jump out of the juke box at any moment'.

So, when the call came that we were to support Howlin' Wolf, who also featured Hubert Sumlin on guitar, you can imagine the trepidation with which we approached this gig – a heady mixture of intense fear and enormous excitement that is the fuel for many a live performer. There was no dressing room at Klook's Kleek; you got changed in an unused industrial-style kitchen. No seats, mirror, toilets or places to hang your clothes apart from those overhead bars which probably had held a sheep's carcass sometime in the distant past. Oh, the glamour of it all. Figuring that if Mr Wolf wouldn't complain, then neither should I.

Hubert Sumlin was the thinnest guitar-playing person currently on the planet. During games of hide and seek he only had to turn sideways to become virtually invisible. He made Flat Stanley seem obese. But he played brilliantly on a blue and white plastic sparkly finished Hagstrom guitar. I loved him. In a manly way, of course.

The hour of performance drew ever closer. Howlin' Wolf was an impressive figure. Dressed in a long black overcoat that he kept on till the last moment, he exuded power. He was short and stocky with a neck twice as wide as Hubert's head. Oh God, how … just how am I going to address him? 'Howlin'' seemed a little too familiar. Should it be 'Mr Wolf?' What if he thought I was taking the piss and pretending to be Little Red Riding Hood? He extended his hand. My heart sank.

'Hi,' he said with a voice like burning gravel. 'My name is Chester, Chester Burnett, nice to meet you.'

There is a God after all.

'Hi Chester,' I stammered. 'Nice to meet you too. We'll be playing with you tonight, and we're really looking forward to it.' Chester shrugged out of his coat, shook himself as if expelling the dust of a thousand bar gigs. Then, taking my hand in both of his, he looked me straight in the eye and smiled, 'I know you guys can play the blues.'

And with that, we took to the stage, our hearts filled with pride that this legend believed in us. And, you know what, we played OK and to quote so many musicians before and those still to come, 'I think we got away with it.' We were just a ragbag collection of students who knew practically nothing, but he encouraged us nevertheless. What a good guy! And Adrian Sumption recalls him inviting us back to Chicago!

We all got on very well and spent time together when we weren't making music. Pete Hocking had Cornish connections and so would take trips to Portscatho in our clapped-out old van. We played the village hall on several occasions, which paid for the trips.

I holidayed with Adrian in Ireland and we hitchhiked all the way, lugging our guitars. A nightmare journey that took twenty-four hours. We were picked up by three inebriated guys in a Jaguar who left us not only in the middle of somewhere in Wales, but also in the middle of the night, where we were eventually rescued by a farmer driving a cattle truck. We stayed in youth hostels and with people we met along the way and there was much imbibing of Guinness and home-brewed hooch. We also attended a Yardbirds gig in Dublin.

Unfortunately, our band wasn't together for very long. Our drummer, Pete Hocking, was subsequently poached by Ronnie Wood to join his band the Birds. Pete later became a shrimp boat captain in Australia, which was an unusual second profession – even for drummers. Adrian, who was studying a degree in engineering, was in his last year when his parents felt he should concentrate on his 'finals' and he quit the band. Adrian is a lovely bloke, with whom I am still in touch – he became a broadcast project engineer at Thames Television before retiring and now volunteers with adults with special needs.

So, the Dissatisfied Blues Band was looking for a drummer. We had seen this guy Andrew Steele playing at the Marquee with a band called the Herd. He was a brilliant player and extremely posh. I quite liked that he didn't pretend to be from the East End of London, just so he would have more street cred (see Mick Jagger).

I guess he had been educated at some expensive school and it felt like he should have been at Sandhurst Royal Military Academy.

Anyway, Andrew moonlighted with our little blues band and we were much better for it. Needing a temporary place to stay he moved into the spare room in my mum and dad's house. He then received a call from legendary producer Joe Meek who needed a drummer for the Tornados. Yes, those Tornados, the group that had the first number one hit, 'Telstar', simultaneously on both sides of the Atlantic. His drums were in the bandwagon which is parked in my parents' drive.

'Any chance you could give me a ride over to Joe Meek's studio at 304, Holloway Road?' asked Andrew.

'Yeah sure, I'm not doing anything this afternoon, happy to help out.'

So off we go and arrive at what turns out to be a maisonette above a ladies' handbag shop on Holloway Road. Joe is a slightly dishevelled person with a limp handshake and a furtive manner. There are no other musicians for Andrew to play with, so he feels if I jam with him it will be more interesting. Joe agrees and so we set up in what would have been the living room. Before we begin, Joe goes upstairs and is gone for quite a while. Bored, I wander into the adjoining room where there are a bunch of reel-to-reel tape recorders and a lot of other strange and mysterious bits of equipment neatly fitted onto some industrial style shelves.

'What the fuck are you doing in here! Get out now! You're never supposed to come in. No one is going to steal my secrets!' yells Joe from the doorway.

'Weird,' I thought to myself.

Andrew and I jam for a while, slightly confused by the whole set-up until Joe tells us he's had enough.

'OK, pack your things away,' he says. 'And you,' he nods in my direction, 'come with me.'

'Now what?' thinks I.

We step into the kitchen.

'He's a bloody good drummer, your mate.'

'Yes, he is.'

'But I don't like him.'

'Oh.'

'Too clever and brainy.'

'Ahh.'

'But you ...'

'Oh shit.'

'You're OK, so do you want to join the Tornados?'

'I didn't even know you were looking for someone.'

'Well we're not now, are we?' he said with a sly look in his eyes.

I lasted about six months. It was my first pro job and I hadn't a clue what I was doing. It was difficult as the group were on their last legs, playing some down-market gigs, but it gave me a taste of being a professional musician. And I learned how to play Greig's 'Hall of the Mountain King', so it wasn't a complete waste of time.

I first met Robert Cromwell Anson in 1965, although he wasn't Robert Cromwell Anson at that time. He had previously changed his name to Phil Kinorrra, when he became a jazz drummer and played with the Don Rendell Quintet and the Brian Auger Trinity. Now that he wanted to be a singer, he was known as Julian Covey. (He later became Philamore Lincoln – he's had more aliases than 'Machine Gun' Kelly and 'Legs' Diamond.) Anyway, I joined his band, Julian Covey and the Machine, which was managed by the Moody Blues' office in Mayfair. It was an intimidating office with a very posh set-up. Cliff Barton, an excellent bass player, was in the band for a short time but left to join the Alan Price Set. Tragically Cliff died from septicaemia due to heroin addiction in 1968, aged just 24.

Julian called me one day and asked me would I like to go to Ghana.

'Are you kidding? Yes of course, what's the deal?'

'There is this guy whose name is Ramon Bouche and he's a piano player who sings a bit. He comes from Ghana and although he is living here, he's a bit of a celebrity over there. He's asked me to help him put a band together to play on a variety show in Accra. It's the inauguration of the Ghanaian television service.'

'Blimey, that sounds amazing.'

'Yes, it should be fun, all expenses paid and £10 fee.'

Well, it was 1965.

This was to be my first time on an aeroplane, my first time out of the country and my first time on television. We met at Heathrow Airport and I was introduced to this tall, gangly, blond-haired bass player called Chris. For some reason we decided to call him Alice. He had the last laugh on us as his surname was Squire and he became the legendary bass player in Yes.

Following in the footsteps of all great musicians, we didn't bother with any rehearsals, figuring we could sort it out when we got there. We flew first class on BOAC in a jet called a Comet. Possibly named because it habitually crashed into the Earth. They put us in an old British colonial-style building named the Ambassador Hotel which was quite splendid. I was vaguely surprised everything was not in black and white as it felt like we were in some movie starring Humphrey Bogart. Lacking any knowledge of how to behave in a hotel of this elegance, we didn't tip anybody. Consequently, by the third day, nobody in the restaurant would serve us. This was rather annoying as, being an all-expenses-paid job, this was the only place we could eat. It seemed you can become the Invisible Man without having to wrap yourself from head to toe in toilet paper. Someone eventually showed us the error of our ways and, from then on, we took great care of them and dined as kings instead of the paupers that we really were.

We thought we ought to sample the local dope, so we found some chap who insisted on taking us to his dealer. One night, we were led off into the ghetto in search of a one shilling bag of grass. Our guide took us down narrow, dark, smelly alleyways between rusting corrugated-iron shacks. Deeper and deeper we went, twisting and turning so much we had no idea how to find our way back. There was only the light of the flashlight carried by our guide. Like lambs to the slaughter. What were we thinking of? Didn't musicians always have the dealer come to them? But let's be honest, we were just a bunch of overgrown children who were so wet behind the ears that a Bedouin tribe could have survived there for months.

Eventually we stopped at a curtain, masquerading as a door. Our guide, Harry (not his real name) banged on the tin wall, risking demolishing the entire shantytown. A wide grin and some white eyes appeared in the doorway.

'Hi Harry, what's happening man?'

'These guys are playing with Ramon Bouche and they're looking to score some weed.'

'Great, come on in.'

We stepped inside the tiny space and he reached up to a shelf and took down an old red tin box with Oxo written on it. He prised it open, revealing about a dozen little baggies made from screwed up white paper. They looked like those little bags of lavender old ladies hung up in their wardrobes to keep the moths away.

'How much you need?' he asked in a very friendly manner. 'They're a shillin' each.'

'We'll take the lot,' says Julian in an instant. Quite entrepreneurial of him I thought. Bring some back to London and make a large profit.

The main worry about this whole adventure was that now they had our money. We needed to get to the hotel without them taking the drugs back. But that turned out to not be a problem, Harry was good as gold. He guided us confidently through the shanties and safely back to the hotel. It was only then that we realised how dangerous it could've been. One word to the police and we could have been locked up in a Ghanaian prison for who knows how long …

The TV show is a bit of a blur so many years later, but I remember thinking the guys operating the cameras knew about as much as us about scoring dope.

The pianist, Dave Levy, really looked after me. He was living in Shepherd's Bush and I recall the flat's ceiling was covered in egg cartons, so he could play the piano without disturbing the neighbours.

He pushed my playing along, but I still couldn't understand why people wanted to work with me. I wasn't that comfortable with my ability but was beginning to realise that I had something, but I felt I was out of my depth. I stayed with Julian Covey (or whatever his name was by then) for a year and learned a lot.

I then joined a band known as the Ingoes. It was really Brian Godding's band. He was a very talented guitarist and a proper song-writer. We played Tamla Motown plus rock and soul, occasionally interspersed with our own songs. The background to the band is interesting and described by rock historian Bruno Ceriotti as:

> Undoubtedly one of the more interesting British psyche-delic groups of the late 1960s, Blossom Toes emerged from a London based semi-pro rhythm 'n' blues beat group called The Gravediggers. In 1964, they were resident at the legendary 2 I's Coffee Bar, alternating with Screaming Lord Sutch. The band changed their name to The Ingoes, after a lesser known Chuck Berry song titled 'Ingo'.

In November of that year, Mr Giorgio Gomelsky started to repre-sent the band. Giorgio managed the Crawdaddy club in Richmond where the Yardbirds had taken over the Rolling Stones' slot. This is not politically correct and would very likely be libellous if the man was still alive (he died in 2016) but Giorgio Gomelsky was quite bonkers. In a good way. And yet he was one of the most influen-tial people on the scene in the mid-1960s. With his thick Russian accent, untouched by his family's move to Switzerland during the war, two octaves lower than anyone else's, and his Rasputin-era beard, he was a commanding but unlikely figure in the clubs and studios. Giorgio would have boxes of the latest American singles sent to him in London, so he could stay in touch.

How did a Russian-Swiss, multilingual intellectual fall so in love with American blues and soul that he went on to start a management and record company with such diverse artists as jazz singer Ottilie Patterson, fusion guitarist John McLaughlin, trombonist Chris Barber, the Yardbirds featuring three of the best guitar heroes (Beck, Clapton and Page), fashion icon and singer extraordinaire Julie Driscoll and psychedelic pop-rockers? Giorgio was a true Renaissance man, flew biplanes during his national service, a film-maker, impresario and songwriter, TV host and disc jockey. Most of all, he truly loved musicians and art.

In 1965, Giorgio instigated the departure of Eddie Lynch with whom Brian Godding had a songwriting partnership and I was his replacement. Brian wasn't best pleased initially, but we got on and I was soon accepted as part of the band. In November of that year, we released a single, in Italy, 'Se Non Mi Aiuti Tu' – a cover of the Beatles' 'Help!' sung in Italian! Useless!

The Ingoes had played in Paris before I joined them, but now we were booked to play at Le Bilboquet, a very small private club, with a tiny stage and dance floor. Visiting musicians, playing at the Paris Olympia or other big venues, would generally show up there after the gig. I remember Bob Dylan sitting on a sofa about 10ft away from the stage. Dressed entirely in black, his trademark black curls piled on top of his head, he might just have come from the album cover shoot for *Blonde on Blonde*. Promoter James Arch opened a new venue and asked us to play there. The Ingoes ended up working for three months, seven nights a week as the resident band. It was to become a much-celebrated club called the Le Bus Palladium and is still going strong. Established during la belle époque, it had been, at various times, a casino, a restaurant called Princesses and even Le Cotton Club, named after the original one in Harlem. From 1929, they hosted artists as renowned as Louis Armstrong and Sidney Bechet. When we first played there, the clientele was beatniks, hippies, drunks, drug addicts, and ladies of the night, before attracting celebs and even aristocracy. After a few weeks, queues to the entrance stretched around the block and among the visitors were Jane Fonda, Baron Lima, the 'King of the Gypsies' and Gregory Peck.

On one occasion when we were playing at a private party and being treated as guests (not always the case), I met the Duke of Windsor when he was next in line for the buffet. By then that was all he was next in line for – having given up being king many years previously, in order to marry the American divorcee Wallis Simpson.

'All right yer holiness?' I was tempted to ask, always probing for a sense of humour, but that ingrained class system that we wrestle with in Britain leapt out and tied a knot in my tongue.

'Are you enjoying yourself?' the duke murmured sociably.

'I was, until I realised you seemed to have some dealings with the Nazis during World War II,' I wanted to say ... but instead, tragically responded, 'Yes, thank you.'

Wankers. Both of us.

One night, Salvador Dali turned up and enjoyed himself so much that he became a regular attendee. Simply meeting him was an overwhelming experience. First of all, his appearance was radically different from anyone else's. The waxed moustache was so large and curved it seemed like an exotic creature resting beneath his nose. Years later, when I was on tour in Florida, I went to the Dali Museum in St Petersburg. For the first time in my life, I used an electronic guide and realised although I have been a fan of his work since art school, I had missed so much. One of those rare occasions where the word genius is aptly applied.

During the month's engagement in the spring of 1966, we stayed at the Hotel Crystal in Saint-Germain-des-Prés, right opposite the Bilboquet club. The gigs began at 9 p.m. and ended at 3 a.m., although we obviously weren't playing continuously. Occasionally we would get to hang out with some of the visitors. Brian Jones from the Stones and Keith Moon from the Who both ended up with us after hours. Jones and I eventually went to Birdland which didn't open till 3 a.m. It was reputedly the very first 'discotheque' and was famous for its chilli con carne. They only played jazz there and the album currently playing had the cover in a spotlight displayed prominently on a table. I guess Le Patron got tired of people asking who was playing. He would give a Gallic shrug and with practised Parisian indifference, indicate the album sleeve.

I liked Brian Jones a lot. We talked about art and living in Paris. I pretended to know something about both of the subjects. He didn't seem to mind as we were both seriously over-refreshed. We had a friend in common, Tara Brown, who I had met a few times, hanging out in Paris. Being a musician, you certainly find yourself in situations that are so far away from your original roots you have to pinch yourself.

We were essentially broke most of the time. Any money we had, we spent on clothes. I guess this was one of the reasons people thought we were successful. And in terms of popularity, we certainly were. But as many musicians will tell you, the illusion of success is just that.

We were invited to play at Chez Maxime, a really famous and expensive restaurant. God only knows what they were thinking of when they hired us. We were never going to be music for fine dining. There was a minuscule dance floor set up just in front of the tiny stage and inebriated clients could stagger into the band, often knocking the microphone stand, so the mic smashed into your mouth. Under the circumstances you became adept at dodging incoming drunks. I remember a portly Peter Ustinov cavorting dangerously with a young lovely and wondering what it would be like to lose a tooth to such an icon. Fortunately, for both of us, we never found out. We really didn't like the place or how we were treated, so seeking revenge, and knowing we would never return, we filled the open spaces on the backs of our Vox AC 30 amplifiers with bottles of wine and cognac that were stored in racks in a corridor leading to the exit. Stolen wine, like kisses, somehow tastes better.

Millionaire playboy Gunter Sachs appeared in front of me just as the band was finishing our final set at the Bus Palladium and invited us back to his apartment to play.

'Let me think about it. Yes,' I replied.

He offered us a vast sum of money, probably £50, so clutching a hastily scribbled address on Avenue Foch, we threw our gear into a couple of taxis and set off. The doorman was not too pleased to see us.

'Sod off, you lot. I'm not waking anybody at this time in the morning, it's more than my job's worth,' was the general translation from the French. We feigned indifference.

'OK, that's fine. Monsieur Sachs has already paid us – so as long as you're OK with telling us to go away, we will go home to bed. Thanks.'

Of course, we didn't care about playing but Gunter was married to Brigitte Bardot and just getting to stand next to her was every schoolboy's dream. In we went. The joint was jumping. We were welcomed with enthusiastic whoops and even a smattering of applause, although sadly not much more than somebody scoring a single run on a hot afternoon at a village cricket match. So, we set the gear up in a corner but before we could play, some young enthusiasts asked if they could have a go.

'Knock yourselves out,' I replied and soon a lot of amateur players had commandeered the instruments and started bashing away.

Brilliant! The place was jammed with beautiful women including Brigitte.

What a wonderful reversal of roles. We got to drink, dance and chat up the girls while the millionaires entertained us. We consumed huge amounts of champagne, imagined we were charming and erudite, whatever that means, and for a couple of hours we felt like all our fantasies were about to be fulfilled. I introduced myself to Brigitte and kissed her on both cheeks. She smelled like vanilla ice cream.

I would love to report otherwise but despite our best efforts, these girls soon realised that any bulges in our trousers were certainly not from overstuffed wallets. We went home at dawn with the clear understanding that although we had rubbed shoulders with the ultra-rich, not a centime had been removed.

Neither had our trousers.

C'est la vie!

We were much in demand the whole time we were in Paris and played a few other venues. We backed Chuck Berry at the Olympia. I recall that his instructions were pretty straightforward.

'When I raise my foot, like so,' he raised a size 15 small watercraft, 'and bring it down like this, you stop.' He then glared at the band and added somewhat threateningly, 'Don't fuck up!' Chuck rarely brought his own band, finding it financially more rewarding to pick up musicians in each town and if he didn't like the way you played, he would simply send you off the stage. Ultimate humiliation. There would be no rehearsal, no set list and no warning in which key the next song would be played. After the show I saw Chuck sitting quietly at the end of the little backstage bar. I walked over and told him what an honour it was to have played with him and I held out my hand. He looked up from his beer, glanced at me coldly and turned away. The ultimate blank. A dismal moment.

Some lunatic thought it would be a good idea to bring the current crop of nightclub acts to French Morocco for a tour. I think it was called something like 'Cabaret De Paris.' Quel Horreur! We were headlining over a magician, some woman singing like Edith Piaf with an accordion and a shrieking cat. We were there for two weeks and it felt like three months. Casablanca was fun. That's probably because we were transported to a belly dancing restaurant where we were forced to get up and dance with semi-naked ladies. Everybody was stoned. The theatre crew constantly smelled of hash. Brian Godding and I would attract hordes of children, who would follow us through the Kasbah like two demented pied pipers. The locals had never seemingly seen the likes of us before – he with his blond hair and me with my red curls.

We travelled from town to town and were allocated an old Chevrolet Bel Air estate car together with a bonkers driver, Mustapha, who we reckoned must have been thrown out of the Gestapo for being too cruel. He seemed to fancy himself as some sort of Moroccan Jackie Stewart. In some stretches, whilst travelling across the open desert, the roads were dead straight for miles, but only one lane wide – about the width of a footpath through a local park. Mustapha hurled the Bel Air down the centre of the path at 80mph. One afternoon, we were hurtling along and, in the distance, but getting closer very quickly, was a cloud of dust thrown up from a fast-approaching truck. Mustapha, who, delighted in this game of 'chicken', scared us witless and probably shitless. Both he and the truck driver held their centre line until the very last microsecond when both vehicles swerved into the gravel-strewn hard shoulder, narrowly averting death for all of us. I suppose the most tragic element would have been that the French chanteuse would have been topping the bill from then on.

It was quite an amazing trip; we were treated so well by the friendly locals. We mainly played village halls and would find ourselves in far-flung outposts, playing to a very mixed crowd – most notable were members of the Tuareg, a semi-nomadic Saharan tribe, who stood at the back encased in their desert robes, their piercing blue eyes contrasting dramatically against their dark outfits. They had travelled by camel to our gig. That had never happened at the Railway Hotel. The Tuareg didn't clap but watched silently and respectfully. They had no idea of what we were doing there – and neither had we.

When we returned to London, the band's name was changed to Blossom Toes. It was Hamish Grimes, a guy who worked for Gomelsky's Paragon Publicity management company, who gave this name to the band, for no good reason or no bad one either. The management office was dominated by a modern recliner, all orange leather and chrome and the couch was dominated by Hamish, whose job it seemed was to stretch out on the said recliner for hours on end and think of new ideas.

Giorgio had Sonny Boy Williamson living in his house for a long time. Sonny Boy was one of the most famous of the bluesmen as he had hosted his own *King Biscuit Show* on KFFA in in Arkansas since 1941. Giorgio would often invite us to come to the house and check through the latest music as part of our education. It was hard to get used to a very tall, thin, black guy, sometimes wearing a bowler hat, or pyjamas, randomly playing harmonica in the kitchen. Sonny Boy appeared to have one side of his upper set of teeth missing and although he was always pleasant, we were definitely in awe of him as he was the real deal. We were just out of our teens and had been playing blues for only a couple of years. Sonny Boy had socks older than us. Rubbing shoulders with a genuine blues man was surreal. It wasn't that we weren't impressed with Clapton or Beck, but we saw them more as rivals, albeit much further up the ladder of success than us, but Sonny Boy …

I masqueraded as a student of architecture, visited an estate agent and took over an elegant, four-bedroom townhouse in Fulham's Holmead Road. Giorgio paid the rent and would later invite visiting Americans over to show how 'hippies lived'. The property was owned by a Greek family who had moved back home. The walls were pale pink, we had pale green carpets from Casa Pupo (the trendiest furniture and design shop at the time), an effervescently emerald, velvet, antique Chesterfield, and we used other silk sofas as beds. I suppose you could call the décor 'Psychedelic Renaissance'.

It was, sadly, soon transformed without any effort into a shabby shell of a place – a notorious hangout for musicians and our 'acquaintances'. At one time, we had as many as twenty-two people staying overnight in the house. Random wandering visitors included Stevie Winwood, Family, Eric Clapton, Captain Beefheart, Eric Burdon and most of the Animals. General shenanigans and noise eventually caused the neighbours to move, which, selfishly, worked to my advantage as my girlfriend moved in to their place. I had met Julia Sachon at the Speakeasy, where she worked as a waitress. She hailed from West Germany, and at 28, was eight years older than me. I suppose she was the closest I ever got to a 'Mrs Robinson' experience. Sadly, our relationship didn't last long and I have to admit she did far better without me. She ended up marrying Peter J. Swales, former Rolling Stones record company executive turned intellectual and described as 'a self-styled punk historian of psychoanalysis'.

According to Charlie Gillett:

Giorgio Gomelsky negotiated with EMI one of the first contracts which gave substantial control and ownership of an artist's recordings to the artist's manager ... he and his fellow managers contributed to a fundamental change in the structure of the British record industry. They really did institute a permanent shift in the balance of power in the British record industry.

However, not all his ideas were that clever. One of his visions for the Ingoes was to promote the band as cartoon characters. The Monkees had been a great success and he thought it would help to create some media interest. But all it did was to piss off the band. He would, on occasions, see himself as some sort of Svengali, but this time none of us wanted to play Trilby.

For most of 1967, Blossom Toes consisted of drummer Kevin Westlake – a sweet character and great musician, who also later joined Ronnie Lane's Slim Chance on guitar – Brian Belshaw played bass and Brian Godding, who was a very talented songwriter and guitarist. I loved being on stage whereas Brian had some moments when he didn't like performing. Blossom Toes wrote and jammed together but we didn't play a gig for ages. Management paid us a retainer of £20 a week which is quite dangerous. Not only did it diminish the hunger sometimes needed for creativity ... it also provided a regular diet of acid, hash and wine. We had stage clothes made and indulged in all the hype associated with the showbiz side of music. I was 21 and liked Pierre Cardin gear. I suppose I was a bit of a flash git.

Giorgio promised us success and we started to write songs and make records. We eventually started gigging and began to record the stuff we played onstage. October 1967 saw the release of our debut single, 'What On Earth / Look At Me I'm You/ Mrs Murphy's Budgerigar.'

Giorgio produced the first Blossom Toes album, *We Are Ever So Clean*. We cut some of the tracks live ourselves but they were then overdubbed with brass and strings. A few tracks were exclusively session musicians including Jimmy Page and Alan White. We weren't best pleased to be ousted from our own record as we thought correctly that we could play well enough to make a reasonable job of it. Months of gigging all night in Paris had given us a certain amount of skill. A few songs were wrecked by arranger David Whittaker but here and there were some signs of budding talent. Mostly from Brian Godding. *Melody Maker* described it as 'Giorgio Gomelsky's Lonely Hearts Club Band'.

A bit annoying as we didn't hear Sergeant Pepper's till ours was finished but not yet in the shops. It did receive some cult status, surprisingly, and was included in *Record Collector*'s list of the '100 Greatest Psychedelic Records'. I've heard that original vinyl versions of the album change hands for as much as £700. At the time, though it wasn't a success at all.

In the summer of 1967, we played at the Love In Festival at Alexandra Palace, on the bill with Eric Burdon and the Animals, Pink Floyd, Brian Auger, Julie Driscoll and the Trinity, and the Crazy World of Arthur Brown. It was an all-nighter, commencing at 9 p.m. and going on to 9 a.m. the following day, and attended by 10,000 people. We were a bit of a shambles, trying to play some of the orchestral arrangements from the record. I thought there was a power cut near the end of the set and so we finished chanting 'Love Us Like We Love You' to a tambourine rather than playing the instruments. Brian Godding, however, recalled that actually the band did not have a power failure, but just ran out of things to play because it was one of our first gigs with the new name and the new line-up, and so we were a little under-rehearsed! It was true that we were under-rehearsed – although no one could accuse us of being under-dressed. Before the festival we'd visited Bermans, the theatrical costumiers, for various outlandish costumes and I had chosen an embroidered, pseudo-Elizabethan doublet – I looked as if I'd just stepped off Sir Francis Drake's *Golden Hind*.

In August that summer, we appeared at the seventh National Jazz, Rock & Blues Festival at the Royal Windsor racecourse. We rarely played the new songs live and so we were a bit spotty but were being pushed hard by 'the management'. We should have played more clubs before we played the festivals. On our second record, we rebelled and didn't enlist the help of session musicians or arrangers and played everything ourselves, which made live performances much more comfortable. That autumn, Kevin Westlake left the band to pursue a solo career – he'd been frustrated in his songwriting aspirations and was replaced by multi-instrumentalist Poli Palmer.

The year of 1968 witnessed some startling events: the Tet Offensive in the Vietnam War; the Prague Spring; Martin Luther King and Bobby Kennedy were assassinated; French students rioted in Paris; Richard Nixon was elected as US President and Blossom Toes started the year with a memorable gig at the Hotel Martinez, Cannes. We were on the same bill as Captain Beefheart and his Magic Band. For some reason, they didn't have any equipment, so they borrowed ours.

Beefheart was one of the regulars at the Blossom Toes abode when he was in town. He seemed to be always on acid. I remember him standing in the doorway to the living room on a number of occasions, with his head pressed to the wall, very close to the light fitting and his finger on the switch, pressing ever so gently until it clicked … at which point he let out an orgasmic sigh. We would become almost as equally entranced, staring at him for an interminable amount of time, waiting for that magical click.

We appeared at the eighth Annual Golden Rose of Montreux Television Festival, with Crazy World of Arthur Brown, Brian Auger and Fairport Convention. The festival was filmed and broadcast live across the nation. Fame at last! In the autumn we were on the bill, along with Jefferson Airplane, the Doors and Terry Reid at the Roundhouse in London. Because of the size of the venue, it wouldn't have been a big pay day, so instead of arguing about money, the bands argued about billing.

There was a major kerfuffle between the Doors and Airplane about which band would close the show. I can't recall whether it was Jim's mob or Grace's bunch who came out on top, but I do remember Blossom Toes were playing in between their sets – so I reckon we can say that the Doors or Airplane were supporting us! In any case, this effect bamboozled the crowd into thinking we were great, and we received a wonderful response. For us it was a taste of success.

In October of that fateful year, Poli Palmer left the band to join Family and was replaced by drummer Barry Reeves. The following month, we were on a bill with Fairport Convention and the surrealistically riotous Bonzo Dog Doo-Dah band.

I was to come across one of the Bonzos, 'Legs' Larry Smith, some years later while on an Elton John tour. Halfway through the set, 'Legs' would appear, dressed in virginal white bridal gown, sporting black capped boots over hairy legs, while on his head was a silver-plated crash helmet, topped with bride and groom figurines from somebody's wedding cake. He demonstrated a well-choreographed tap dance, while Elton played 'I think I'm going to kill myself.' Now that's entertainment.

Dave Jacobsen, our road manager, at the time, was known as S.R., which stood for Super Roadie because he was simply amazing at whatever he did. He was a great sound mixer, set up all our gigs, and did whatever needed doing. Everyone loved him. One night, our dressing room was raided. I think it was in Scunthorpe, but it may have been somewhere even less salubrious. The police found a little bit of hash belonging to Dave. A tiny amount – what was known then as 'a £1 deal'. He was on probation for some other misdemeanour, and, so to protect him and prevent him from being sent down, all the members of the band pleaded guilty to possession. We each received suspended sentences. Funnily enough I don't have that on my record any longer and have only been charged with one other offence – trashing a hotel room in Florida … as you'd expect.

In May 1969 Harvey Bramham, Fairport Convention's road manager and sound technician, was driving the transit van and fell asleep at the wheel. The band's drummer, Martin Lamble, was killed along with Jeannie Franklyn, Richard Thompson's girlfriend. Harvey, who was a friend of mine, never recovered from this terrible tragedy. We played a benefit for the band at the Roundhouse along with Pink Floyd, Pretty Things, Family and Mick Fleetwood. A few months later, our second album, *If Only for a Moment*, was released and we also appeared at a couple of national blues festivals at Windsor and Plumpton racecourses among other places.

I've always been an enormous fan of Frank Zappa. I went to see him and the Mothers of Invention at the Albert Hall in the late 1960s. The Mothers kicked off by repeatedly playing just one beat on one note. A deafening rhythmic tonal stomp. Meanwhile the London Philharmonic Orchestra started playing. Of course, you couldn't hear them at all but you could see the string players sawing away. Zappa stood centre stage with both arms spread wide. He tilted them like an airplane making a steep banking turn. High up on the band side and lower on the orchestra side.

Slowly he started to level out his arms. The band grew quieter and quieter under his direction and as the tilt of his arms was reversed, you started to hear the strings. As the melody dawned on the audience they burst into applause. They were playing Ravel's *Bolero*. This continued for a while till Frank raised up the band again and drowned them out.

Brilliant! Such a cheeky thing to do. Don Preston then climbed up through the tiered seats to the 'mighty, majestic Albert Hall pipe organ' and thumped out 'Louie, Louie' and the place went wild.

In October 1969 we played at the Festival Actuel, a five-day event in the Belgian village of Amougies. It turned out that the master of ceremonies was Zappa himself. He introduced us and, a few songs in, we were playing a psychedelic tune, 'The saga of the frozen dog', with a kind of atonal backing track. The next thing I know, Frank is standing next to us, joining in on the solos and then giving us the nod to swap eight bars. I was mesmerised – I couldn't believe I was jamming on stage with one of my heroes. I expect it was quite a fiasco to listen to, but I really enjoyed those five to ten minutes. He took a bow and we thanked him afterwards. He was very complimentary about our band and that knocked me out. I've always loved his work.

That appearance was the highpoint of my time with Blossom Toes. I felt that there was so much more to come, but sadly a couple of months later it was all over. In December 1969 with just the band in a car on our way back from a gig at Bristol University, our Volkswagen Beetle (what else) hit some black ice on the M4. We overturned and ended up upside down in the fast lane of the oncoming traffic. One car was unable to avoid us and hit our vehicle. We spun like a top. Fortunately, it was late at night and there was very little other traffic on the motorway. Miraculously, nobody was seriously injured, although we were very shaken up and were off the road for a while. Apparently, Brian Auger was so upset and sympathetic, he gave the band £200 to go away for two weeks to regroup. I say 'apparently' because I didn't see any of the dosh and as soon as I've finished this chapter, I'll be getting on to Mr Auger about what has happened to my share, which I've worked out is now worth approximately £560.32. In any case Brian Godding and Brian Belshaw decided not to carry on and the band split up. Barry Reeves went off to Germany and joined the James Last Orchestra.

I was incredibly disappointed as the band were selling out every-where and on the verge of great success. I had to start all over again.

3

Setting the Cat on Fire

What do you call a guitarist without a girlfriend?

Homeless.

It was Shawn Phillips who first turned me on to LSD. He was an interesting American folk-rock singer, who had lived with Donovan in the 1960s and played sitar on one of his records. Shawn had served in the navy briefly before devoting his life to music, and later becoming a voluntary marine fireman (a rescue scuba diver) in Houston while still recording albums. I've done all of that as well – apart from being in the Senior Service, co-habiting with Donovan and firefighting.

Anyway, in 1970, Shawn had a flat in Chelsea where we hung out and where we all used to turn on, and probably tune out as well – I've also probably dropped out on occasions without realising it. For my first acid trip, about eight of us sat around encircling a huge candle, while listening to traditional Indian music and Shawn reading extracts from *The Tibetan Book of the Dead*. (And long before Richard Gere got the idea for an audiobook.) Shawn acted as a kind of spirit guide. This was a serious event – not to be taken lightly.

I regularly experimented with acid during that time and it really did help me experience feelings and emotions I had not yet discovered – although once I discovered them, I wasn't always clear what to do with them. But I sincerely felt that I could discover the meaning of life and the drug did put me in touch with what appeared to be God or some kind of spiritual being. I haven't done acid for years and wouldn't recommend using it. LSD can be dangerous if you don't know where it has come from, what you're doing with it or if you're not in a safe place with people you trust.

Shawn and I became good mates and he invited me to Positano where he had his own studio apartment right at the top of the mountainside village and access to a flat above his where I could stay. Apart from the lure of an Italian seaside residence, he also wanted me to write some music for a forthcoming play that Peter Sellers was to appear in at the Roundhouse.

At the time, my girlfriend was Krista, a Belgian photographer, who I had met at a gig. She was lovely, and we shared a flat in Clapton. The only problem was that she didn't like it when I wasn't in London and she was left on her own. So, you can imagine, being in a relationship with a rock musician wasn't exactly ideal for her, as a lot of the time I was away touring or gigging. It was thus agreed that we would make the trip together to Italy. As soon as Krista and I arrived in Positano, Shawn informed me that, unsurprisingly, Peter Sellers had dropped out of the production and the project was dead in the water ... as was any payment.

Shawn's accommodation was spectacular and had two floor-to-ceiling, Gothic-style windows, looking out across the rooftops and to the Mediterranean below. Our own living space was immediately below Shawn's but without the arched windows. It was approximately 2,600 steps down to the beach and we climbed these surprisingly easily a couple of times a day. I was concerned I was channelling my inner mountain goat and that cloven hooves would suddenly start to emerge.

Shawn and I soon took on the mantle of serious mountaineers as we loved to ascend the peak, rising high above the village. On one occasion, as we hauled ourselves up through the ancient remains of terraces – possibly used by the Romans for farming – a mist came down. The visibility was reduced to about 15ft. We could still see what we were doing so we decided to keep climbing. We continued for a considerable amount of time and, just as I was starting to chicken out, we burst through the mist to find ourselves merely a few feet from the very top. There was an enormous metal cross planted at the summit and, above us, the sky was a piercing blue. All around us as far as we could see was cloud and our mountain peak sat up like a tiny island in a sea of cotton wool. You know that moment just when a plane breaks through the clouds? Well it was just like that ... only better.

Being from Texas, where men are men and cows are nervous, Shawn decided that he needed to clamber to the top of the cross. With the assault course skill befitting an ex-marine he swung up on this 15ft religious icon and straddled the crossbar. Holding on to the top of the upright pole, with his waist-length blond hair streaming behind him, he waved one arm in the air like a rodeo rider on acid and yelled, 'Yippee!'

This was 'shock and awe' as portrayed by someone from the Lone Star State. Two thousand years of Christianity down the drain. Eventually, we sat peacefully in the sun and ate our sandwiches before leaving our island in the clouds, descending through the mist to home.

Positano in the winter was very quiet. We were befriended by some French actors who had rented a large apartment in an old palazzo. It had faded frescoes and slightly battered antique furniture, but it also had a wide terrace where we regularly ate lunch. The cast was Alan Frankel, an American hippy and intellectual, actor Jean-Pierre Kalfon and two beautiful actresses, Valérie Lagrange and Margareth Clémenti, who later appeared in in Fellini's *Casanova* and a couple of other films.

I needed to earn some money … and quickly, so I started busking, accompanied by the two actresses, to bring in a few pence – or should I say a few thousand lire. We rode scooters to Sorrento where there were lots of tourists. After a couple of choruses of 'Blowing in the Wind', Balthazar, Margareth's son, an adorable hippy boy, aged about 6, would ask the gathering crowd for a donation. Before you could say, 'My Ferrari's out of petrol', people were handing out money – no one could say no to him or the beautiful girls.

In no time, we had made enough money to eat lunch in local restaurants and to purchase provisions for the evening. Who knew busking was such good business, now it can even be more lucrative with buskers being able to take money via their iPhones. We had lots of fun; it was a bohemian existence, a very relaxed winter, playing football on the beach (even though I'm no Lionel Messi), devouring spaghetti lunches in the apartment and learning to play chess with Alan. There have been periods in my life when I've had lots of money and other times when I haven't – and, looking back, some of my happiest times were when I had very little.

The gang had stayed in Positano previously and one summer had lived in a rented house on an island between Positano and Capri called Gallo Lungo, part of an archipelago of three islands known as Li Galli. The island was also known as Le Sirenuse (from *sirena* in Italian), a reference to the mythological sirens said to have inhabited the islands, and who lured sailors to their death. The islands were purchased in 1988 by Rudolf Nureyev, who spent some of the last years of his life in a seven-suite villa.

One day, Valérie mentioned that she and some others had formed a band on the island and she thought there were still some instruments left in the house. My ears pricked up.

'Really, what sort of instruments?'

'Well, I know there is a drum kit and maybe a guitar,' she said in that beautiful voice softly tinged with a French accent.

'Any chance we could go and see?' I tried not to salivate at the chances of getting hold of some instruments other than just the one I had brought with me from London.

'Yes, all we need to do is ask one of the fishermen to take us over there.'

'Great! Let's go and look ...'

So, soon after, and with a complete lack of heed to health and safety, Valérie, Margareth, Alan and I commandeered an open skiff and set off from the jetty. It wasn't the best of days to do this. The Mediterranean can be quite bad tempered when it feels like it. To the fishermen, this was just a gentle breeze but to us the white caps and the cold spray were a little unnerving. Undaunted, we ventured across a stormy sea, battling the waves before landing safely on a sheltered, albeit rocky, landing place where we were able to tie up before going exploring. Fortunately, we saw no sirens, but at the house there were a couple of visions: an orange sparkly Ludwig drum kit, and even more of a find was a Gibson ES 350T guitar – a monstrously great guitar and often seen on Chuck Berry LP covers.

Before loading these treasures onto the boat Valérie asked me if I wanted the island tour. The two of us explored this beautiful isle and as we walked it seemed to me that we were both getting as close to each other as possible. I wanted to hold her hand or put my arm around her, but I thought of my girlfriend Krista, back in the village, so I managed to restrain myself. I was, however, smitten by Valérie. She radiated this calm elegance that, combined with her natural easy charm and stunning beauty, was an undeniably potent force.

In fact my relationship with Krista was by now falling apart. I wasn't sure why. This had nothing to do with Valérie, as I had felt a little trapped before Krista and I came to Positano. I felt she had become a bit too co-dependent and wasn't very good at being alone. Impossible, given my work. I had suggested that she take on more photography projects whenever I was away. I know it's hard to be the one left behind when your partner goes on the road but you have to learn to be comfortable in your own skin. Krista was an unusual combination of being both independent and insecure.

I've always been drawn to independent women who want to pursue their own careers. This can be a double-edged sword. If you choose someone who can stand on their own two feet and be as forceful as you, there is always the chance that they might find that they don't need you. But isn't that part of the attraction? Sometimes when you return from a long tour, your partner has managed so well on their own, that you may find you feel like a stranger in your own home. It doesn't last, but it's unsettling. Still, I seem to need a partner who challenges me. It doesn't matter how sexy, beautiful or successful the woman might be, it's inevitable that as the excitement of the initial attraction wears off, there must be something else, hopefully leading to something deeper like love and devotion.

I digress – not for the first time distracted by gorgeous women. We transported these instruments back and I played on the drum kit most mornings before breakfast, covered in tea towels so as not to annoy the neighbours. I was – and you'll just have to believe me – the Charlie Watts of tea towel drummers.

As for the Gibson? I played it lovingly for two years until the French bloke who owned it relieved me of it at a gig he coincidentally attended. I mistakenly thought that if I played it better than him, he'd let me keep the guitar. He didn't. It was heart-breaking, and I never replaced it.

Soon after, a man called Kevin Hoidale appeared in Positano. Although a working musician, Kevin was a member of the family who ran the General Mills multinational food company, which owned Kellogg's, Yoplait, Lucky Charms and Betty Crocker, among others. Worth a bob or two. Kevin was in Objectivo, a popular band in Portugal and they now needed a guitarist, so he offered me a job, which I accepted.

I planned to go there via London in order to collect guitars and equipment and Krista and I managed to blag a lift with a beautiful blonde called Marilyn (not that one) who was not only glamorous, but great fun; with her looks and deep booming voice, she was a real head turner. (She later turned the head of Led Zeppelin's tour manager, Richard Cole, and ended up marrying him.) We somehow squeezed into a Porsche 911 that Marilyn had borrowed from her then Arab boyfriend. We didn't have any money to stay anywhere and so we took turns driving. It was this trip that accelerated my interest in sports cars – although not from the rear passenger seat!

Alan, Valérie and Margareth had decided to accompany us as far as Naples and so we said our goodbyes to Shawn. I had been very friendly with Valérie, but I was still with Krista and, I have to say, I had behaved unusually well. Alan and I said goodbye to her and Margareth, but immediately afterwards, in a Naples station toilet of all places, Alan tapped me on the shoulder.

'I've got to give you this letter.'

'Thanks, Alan, but could I finish peeing first?'

'No. Well, yes … I guess so. But be quick. It's important.'

'Give me a moment I don't want to get stuck in the zip.'

'Just read the letter.'

Intrigued, I took the envelope, but, of course, only after I had washed my hands.

'It's from Valérie,' Alan muttered. 'She asked me to give it you.'

I was bemused. 'What here … in the toilet?'

'After you said goodbye to her. We just happen to be in the toilet. Just open the Goddamn letter for Chrissake.'

I ripped open the envelope and read the note. Valérie confessed that she had fallen in love with me but had done nothing about it because of Krista. She was heartbroken that I was leaving Positano but didn't want to tell me because she didn't want me to miss my chance of joining the band in Portugal.

I had actually intended to split from Krista when we got back to London. I obviously hadn't mentioned this to Valérie. In fact, I hadn't even mentioned it to Krista. Damn! We men are particularly slow in picking up the signals from the opposite sex. Especially at that age – I was about 22 at the time and Valérie was a few years older than me.

After haranguing Alan for not interrupting my pee earlier, I rushed outside, but Valérie had gone. I had also become besotted with Valérie, and so was over the moon that she felt the same way. I was amazed that such a very beautiful and amazing woman could feel this way about me but devastated that I seemed to have missed my chance to be with her. I sent Valérie a telegram, which read, 'Love is All'. I had no idea what it meant, but it seemed very romantic at the time and there wasn't much else I could do. I thought of her constantly on the journey back and wondered how I was ever going to meet with her again.

We arrived in London, where Krista remained. Our relationship was pretty doomed by then and she met some other guy and moved on. I collected my gear – two guitars, an amp, some cables and suitcases crammed with jeans, and T-shirts – all I possessed in the world and I boarded a boat from Southampton bound for Bilboa. We were met at the port by a guy called Juan, who I assumed was Objectivo's roadie, who then drove us to Estoril – a two-day trip. Kevin Hoidale's home, 'Quinta De Casqulhera', roughly translated as Shell Farm, was set in 40 acres where he and his partner raised Saluki dogs. The pile was extraordinary, with vast rooms, and decorated in an ornate and elegant style. We were advised that the cook and butler would look after us and when we went down for dinner the first night, we were greeted by our driver, who in a transformation that would have graced any decent panto, was now resplendent in dark green, livery uniform, silver buttons fastened to the neck. 'Roadie Juan' had become 'Butler Juan'. So, I'd only gone and poured out all my rock 'n' roll stories and my many indiscretions, which I thought would pass the time in the two-day journey, to the fucking butler. I trusted he would remain inscrutable in the true tradition of butlers.

He proceeded to unlock an ornate chest, lifted out a shoe box and opened the lid to reveal a dizzying array of grass and hash for our delectation. A connoisseur's collection of hashish from all over the world, and of various shades: Afghani black, Lebanese red and Kashmiri green. I bet this was one duty that Jeeves never had to perform while in the employ of Bertie Wooster. Quite a grand lifestyle, which I took to in about thirty seconds.

Kevin's band had their own club where we performed, and we also did a television show and made a record. Objectivo were a nice band, but we weren't going anywhere career-wise. Eventually we were joined by a sax player and we were moved into other digs, which were fine, but nowhere near as palatial as Shell Farm.

It was at this point that Valérie joined me. It was pretty weird. We knew each other as friends, and had declared undying love for each other, but had never even held hands. She arrived by train, and I was waiting for her at the station. Here was this French film star, arriving to be my lover. She was lovely, very gracious, and much more worldly than me. What was this beautiful woman, who had travelled all this way, expecting of me? I was sure I was out of her league and I was scared shitless. In fact, the first night we spent together I was a nervous wreck and not up to anything. She was very understanding.

The time we had spent together in Positano was a bohemian existence, not based in any kind of reality and full of pure, simple enjoyment with no responsibilities or expectations.

We were very happy once we got used to each other and played house together for about six months, and although we were really warm and loving towards each other, the expected sparks didn't quite fly. The added complication was that she had a 12-year old son, living with his father. She obviously wanted to be with her boy and I didn't yet see myself in the role of stepfather. So, Valérie returned to Paris. (Incidentally, for those readers who like loose ends tied up, we met for lunch in Paris many years later and Valérie was just as lovely and gracious as ever.)

Well, Objectivo fell apart and in 1971, I returned to England to get some work. While staying with friends, I worked on an album with a band called Stud, who were the brainchild of drummer John Wilson. Both he and bass player Charlie McCracken had been the powerhouse rhythm section behind Rory Gallagher in Taste, but John had left the band, wanting to play music other than blues. He wanted to be a British Tony Williams and form a band, based on Williams' celebrated group, Lifetime. This British equivalent was to play a mixture of jazz, rock, folk, funk and acoustic – sometimes all at once. Much lunacy ensued.

I've always been quite a good bluffer and I pretended that I knew what I was doing, but I was way out of my depth. John had incredible chops as a drummer and used to suggest unplayable time signatures such as three and two thirds, four or 11/8 which were almost beyond me. It was all a bit of a fiasco at times but having said that, the band were great fun, and we had a small but lunatic following. We toured in Germany (Taste were very big there) and did quite well.

Our manager was Eddie Kennedy, a Belfast club owner and in my opinion, something of a crook. I'd never seen his like before or after in so-called management. We were on a retainer, so Eddie made all the money. We made a recording and his son Billy Kennedy produced the album, although he had never produced anything before. It was all pretty embarrassing and the record didn't do anything.

We made a second album, which was a bit more interesting, but I wasn't enjoying myself and started to get fed up. The band was falling apart and I decided to leave. I told Eddie that I was leaving and wanted to get my stuff out of the band's van and he replied, 'What stuff?'

I replied, 'My equipment, the amps, you know what.'

He tried it on, saying that the gear belonged to the band and wasn't mine. I gave him short shrift and he gave in. A real shyster manager.

Turned out we were even renting the van – we had wrongly assumed that we owned our own transport!

Both John and Charlie are wonderful players and we remain friends. Great guys. Poor old Rory Gallagher died of the drink in 1995. Those Irish guys could drink. I wasn't a world-class drinker but would class myself as a pretty good amateur.

At the time, Poli Palmer and I were sharing a house in Fulham. It was totally abysmal. Poli lived in the basement, which he had done up a little. I had two rooms at the top of the house. There was no bathroom, just a sink in the kitchen, but the toilet, which the whole household shared, was on the landing two floors down. So I was forced to bathe luxuriously at the Fulham Baths in North End Road, a Grade 2 listed building, which is now a dance rehearsal studio. Ahh ... the glamorous rock and roll life ...

In September of 1972 I joined Family. Roger Chapman, their lead singer, had been in need of a bass player a year or two before and I had suggested John Wetton, a family friend from Bournemouth. He was wonderful, and the band were very grateful, but he had now left the group to join Uriah Heep and later King Crimson and the highly successful band Asia. (John, very sadly died from cancer in 2017.)

Charlie Whitney from Family called me out of the blue and said, 'We want you to replace John.'

'I haven't even got a bass,' I offered.

'Ahh ... we've bought you one.'

'Why me for God's sake?' I countered.

'It's your fault. You got John in the band and now he's left so you've got to take his place.'

'Oh all right, but do I get to drive the band's Bentley on days off?'

'Yeah, sure,' came the reply.

And so I did.

Joining the band also gave me the opportunity to re-unite with my old friend Poli.

Family were a pretty big deal at the time and favourites of Elton John. So, when he was planning a thirteen-week tour of the United States he kindly invited us to join him. Magnificent! This was to be my first visit and we were to start off in New York. It had been my dream since I started playing that one day I would be flying there in the guise of a professional musician and at last it was coming true. I couldn't have been more excited and the guys in the band told me it was going to be something I would never forget. And that's absolutely true. As you drive over Brooklyn Bridge and the entire downtown Manhattan skyline is first revealed, is an image I still carry with me. The scale of the buildings is so impressive; you marvel at the ingenuity and brilliance of the architects and planners.

I fell in love with New York immediately. So many British musicians see the United States as their spiritual home. It is after all, the birthplace of jazz, blues and rock. Even though it can be easily argued that Celtic folk music is at the heart of Americana, nearly all my heroes were African Americans: John Coltrane, Miles Davis, Muddy Waters, B.B. King, Ray Charles, Little Richard, and Chuck Berry. And the ladies; Ella Fitzgerald, Mavis Staples, Aretha Franklin, Etta James and Billie Holiday and that's just the list at 12.15 today. Ask me again tomorrow and there would be many more.

So, we launch into this tour playing about a forty-five-minute set and giving it everything we had. Gene Clair, the sound engineer and owner of Clair Brothers sound systems, the absolutely best guy in the business, remarked, 'The trouble is it's as if you're playing a club. You guys are so loud, I can hardly mix it. These big arenas are very echoey, so you need to calm down a bit.'

Fat chance. This is who we are. This is what we do. We are not changing for anybody.

Sadly – and I don't think for the above reason – Family never made it in the States. Not only was our music radically different from Elton's but so was Roger Chapman's voice. Powerful and gritty, Roger's sound was unique. With his wild stage performance and occasionally menacing body language, his appeal was to a tougher crowd.

Elton's band were quite different. Great players, they had more of a studio approach. I guess there's no point hiring Gene Clair if you're not going to listen to his advice. They were seriously good and we would stay and watch Elton and his band most nights, often hanging out backstage drinking Jack Daniels with Bernie Taupin, Elton's co-writer and lyricist extraordinaire. I became friends with Elton and some of his musicians. Guitarist Davey Johnstone is a great player and a lovely guy and is still with the band. Elton's drummer, Nigel Olsson, also a great bloke, went on to race Ferraris. I guess he had two of the jobs that every boy would want.

The tour was very enjoyable, everyone got on and friendships were formed that have lasted years. And the gigs! I got to play Carnegie Hall and Madison Square Garden. Our record company had a publicist called Annie Ivil who came backstage before the Madison Square show. We were understandably nervous.

'Darlings,' she smiled, 'they are going to love you. The New Yorkers are the most brilliant, receptive and generous audience you will find anywhere. You are going to have the best time up there so just relax and have fun.'

And we did.

I will never be able to thank Annie enough for those wonderful lies that gave us the boost of confidence we needed. Her delivery was so convincing that even though somewhere in the back of my mind I knew it was all bollocks, I desperately wanted to believe her.

So, I did.

We travelled by scheduled airlines, so we often had to take two or three flights to get to our destination. Fortunately, this was in the era before hijacking became quite so common, so you just had to be at the airport half an hour before the plane left. Even so it could be tough getting up to catch an 8 a.m. flight; with a couple of changes and some hanging about you might not get to the venue till three or four in the afternoon.

I remember on one occasion when we were queuing up on the jetway waiting for the cleaners to finish when Elton thought it was a perfect time to burst into a number from *West Side Story*. I should point out that it was winter, and he was wearing a pink fur coat. I'm not sure what the other passengers thought as he belted out, 'I feel pretty, Oh, so pretty, I feel pretty and witty and GAYYYYYY!!!' The last word gay was at full volume and in the enclosed space it was fabulously effective.

A certain amount of tour madness occurred. I seem to remember I was continually wearing a big black cowboy hat with a large green fluffy frog pinned by its belly to the crown, its arms and legs flopping around on the brim, whilst the amphibian's blank eyes stared glassily at oncoming pedestrians. Foolish person.

After about six weeks away, singer Linda Lewis, my then girlfriend, came for a short visit. I'm not sure how she arranged this but after a couple of days, the separate truck that was carrying all Family's equipment broke down several miles from the venue. It was impossible to get our gear in time for the show. Elton knew Linda from when she had opened for him on a British tour, so he very sensibly suggested that she go on for half an hour in our place. She was very, very good and completely captivated the audience, accompanying herself on an acoustic guitar. She got two encores and could have stayed for another half hour.

I should point out that Family didn't get any encores during the entire thirteen weeks. Nothing was said, but my overactive imagination thought it heard mutterings from the band; 'Don't bring yer girlfriend next time.'

Bastards.

I only made one record with Family, although I did appear triumphantly on *Top of the Pops* ... albeit miming to John Wetton. Towards the end we were joined by Tony Ashton on keys who was one of the funniest people I have ever met. We toured Europe, but we were running out of steam and decided after a farewell tour to call it quits. However, I did learn a lot from Roger Chapman. He was pretty blunt and so you certainly knew where you stood with him. Roger also takes his music very seriously – his honesty and musical integrity are beyond reproach and the concept of commerciality for its own sake is foreign to him. He also loves his players and gives such freedom to his band. It's very exciting to be on stage with him. You don't know what will happen next.

Roger is a complex character. He could be gentle at times but came from a tough background. He might well have ended up in jail, had it not been for his music. On one occasion I saw his hotel room, which was in a state of complete devastation. I asked him, 'How come I'd missed the party?' 'Oh, there was no party,' he replied. 'I just felt like doing it.' It was the first time I'd ever seen a room trashed by one person.

I've already mentioned her, but it's about time I introduced you properly to my first wife, although of course at that time I didn't know she was going to be my first wife. I met Linda Lewis in the early 1970s at a free music festival at London's Primrose Hill. I had sat in with her group, the Ferris Wheel, in a club in Geneva (Linda had replaced Marsha Hunt in the band for two weeks) and I was immediately smitten by this beautiful, wild, talented girl with amazing hair. It was a while before we got together as we were both in relationships, but then we moved in together to a communal home in Hampstead. Well, I say we moved in together. Needless to say, I was between accommodation and Linda was already ensconced in the lovely house on the edge of the heath and I joined her and the other occupants. The other occupants included style icon 'man about town' and underground DJ, Jeff Dexter; Rhonda, an American escort; record executive Ian Samwell, who wrote Cliff Richard's first hit 'Move it' and 'What'cha Gonna Do About It?' for the Small Faces; and occasional resident mime artist, Toad. I guess, in those days, I would have described it as a sort of 'hippy heaven'.

It was a lovely old house, but only offered one loo which was in the bathroom. So you would be taking a bath, and someone would come in and have a pee. It took me a little while to get used to peeing in front of housemates. Not exactly conducive for young lovers. The other complication was that Linda and Ian had once been 'an item', but they were cool, and it all worked out fine and there were no jealous spats – even in the bathroom.

In truth, the bathroom turned out to have other more important properties. My pal Tony Rowland, an aspiring singer/songwriter, wanted to audition for Jeff and I agreed to play along with him. We both stood in the empty bathtub and serenaded Jeff, who was perched on the loo. Although it was the best room in the house for sound, Jeff still pulled the plug.

The commune was an attractive place for people to drop by and we had lots of visitors. Everyone loved Linda. Cat Stevens and Marc Bolan were regulars as well as members of the band America, who were managed by Jeff. Linda had actually stepped out with Cat Stevens before me. He wrote '(Remember the Days of the) Old Schoolyard' for Linda, who had sung back-up on his 1972 album, *Catch Bull at Four*.

Linda's manager was Tony Gourvish. He used to work the clubs in the mid-1960s when he was known as Tony Esquire and rode a Lambretta. He had arranged for Linda to open for the great Richie Havens on a tour around the UK. Richie's musicians loved Linda – she was just working on her own with an acoustic guitar – and she asked them to make an album with her. The record was called *Lark* and was my first job as a producer. We recorded it at Apple Studios and our engineer was Phil McDonald, who later worked on John Lennon's song 'Imagine'. Musicians loved being in that studio – such was the mystique of the Beatles and, in fact, George, Ringo and Paul used to look in. The studio was the closest thing to Abbey Road in those days.

From the outset, I had ideas about how to produce and have often used the same approach. I like musicians to be fresh when they come in. They don't know what songs they will be recording and in this way, they instinctively respond to each other. In this way the sessions are more organic and spontaneous. Of course, this can be expensive as it takes longer in the studio when the parts aren't all written beforehand, but I've found it to be successful.

And I maintain that the first idea a musician comes up with has exactly the same value as the next. The fifth thought might be the one you eventually prefer, but you shouldn't dismiss the earlier ideas just because they came easily. They arrive without the baggage of deliberation. Quincy Jones is quoted as saying, 'Don't tie the arrangement down so tight that you don't leave space for God to walk through the room!' Let the musicians be themselves. The 'casting' must be right. I know that Bob Dylan and Brian Eno work this way and they seem to have done rather well.

Anyway, *Lark* still stands up. It was Linda's second record and was released in 1972. The album had an innocence that is unique. And we received excellent reviews. Linda's five-octave vocal range attracted much attention – here's what Vince Aletti, *Rolling Stone* journalist, wrote:

> Linda Lewis has this very strange voice. It's like a little girl's: high, with a breathy sort of purity, full of recklessness and wit. But it also has an unexpectedly rough texture which cuts into the little-girl quality so that, while she sounds like no one else, there are moments when she feels like early Stevie Wonder crossed with Michael Jackson – an extraordinary combination.

I also co-produced *Fathoms Deep* and Linda's fourth album, *Not a Little Girl Anymore*, a few years later. The legendary Tower of Power horns wrote the arrangements and played for us. They also wrote the title track and performed it for us to decide if we wanted to cut it. It was quite something to witness large, bearded hunks, singing great harmony with the lyric, 'I'm not a little girl anymore.'

The genius behind Little Feat, Lowell George, guested on one track. We had met him a couple of nights before and he agreed to be on the album. He was delightful. He didn't want any money – just a couple of grams of coke, which someone provided for him. He didn't use an amp, simply plugging his Stratocaster straight in to the console. He crafted the solo in about a minute and a half, stayed for a quick chat and then left. No mess, no fuss.

After a year together in Hampstead Way, Linda and I rented a flat in Arlington Park Mansions in Turnham Green, West London, a fourth-floor walk-up, without a lift. I used to get fed up with climbing all those stairs and one night after much jollity, reached the third floor and thought I'd take a rest. I woke up the next morning at about 8 a.m. with people stepping over me on their way to work. I expect the case of the drunken musician blocking the staircase was duly raised as an agenda item at the residents meeting. 'We've heard of a sitting tenant, but a sleeping tenant?'

Our bed was a mattress on the floor of a tiny room. We had one nice piece of furniture – a Victorian Chesterfield in tan leather with an arm that dropped down to make it into a chaise longue. Linda was stretched out on it one night when she received a phone call from Marsha Hunt. She had just interviewed Stevie Wonder on the radio, who told Marsha that the person he'd most like to meet while he was in UK was … Linda Lewis. Linda got Marsha off the phone quicker than you could say 'Superstition' and rang the number Marsha had given her. Stevie said he was so happy to hear from her and actually sang one of her songs down the phone to her. Linda was in tears. We went to see him at Island Studios the next day. He was mixing a live album and while the tape was rewinding, he would jam on a nearby keyboard. The guy loves music so much; he just has to play at every opportunity. It was amazing. Stevie's a brilliant mimic and would take me off. He was so complimentary about Linda's work and I basked in a bit of reflected glory. A delightful man with a huge sense of humour.

One summer, Mike Batt and his wife Wendy invited Linda and me to join them on their 128ft yacht *Braemar* for a journey across the Atlantic from the Canary Islands to Antigua, in the Caribbean. So we flew down to Tenerife and hopped on board.

'She's older than the *Queen Mary*,' said Mike proudly, 'and still going strong.' I assumed he was talking about the *Braemar* rather than Wendy but, in actual fact, both of them were still in very good condition. We were joined by their two young daughters, Robin and Samantha. Even so, we were outnumbered by the crew. Captain, first officer, first and second engineer, steward, deckhand and, most importantly, cook.

I wasn't particularly taken by Tenerife. Black volcanic sand didn't really work for me, coming as I did from Poole in Dorset, where there are miles of pristine golden sands offset by the freezing waters of the English Channel. Our accommodation on board was beautiful. Finished in what may have been honey-coloured oak, our double bed had those side rails to prevent small children from falling out. Everything was built-in, and later on, I had occasion to wish that we were too.

We set off at sunset and I remember very clearly standing at the stern rail watching the island fade into the distance with about 3,000 miles of open ocean before our next landfall. As we moved away, over the horizon, the sky filled with stars, accentuated by the lack of moonlight. What had appeared like a sizeable yacht when we first stepped aboard, now seemed like a grain of sand in the Sahara desert. There were no birds, ships or aeroplanes and, apart from the occasional sonic boom of Concorde, we were all alone in this vast expanse of water.

We read, talked, played music, made up silly games and generally had loads of fun. Being a semi-professional nautical nuisance, I asked the first officer if he would show me how to work a sextant and introduce me to celestial navigation. He was very helpful and patient. The sextant part was quite easy. It was the calculating bit that floored me – no matter how I tried. According to my calculations, the yacht was generally somewhere outside Pittsburgh deep in mainland USA. Thank God for the invention of sat nav.

People often recount stories of dolphins keeping you company by playing in the bow wave and that was certainly true of this voyage. But one morning, we woke to several orcas doing the same thing.

'Are those killer whales?' a troubled-looking Linda asked.

'No, no, certainly not,' I replied with a carefree grin. 'They are orcas, not the same thing at all. Aren't they beautiful?' I added, doing my best impression of a nonchalant sea dog and failing miserably.

'They bloody well are killer whales. I can tell by the look on your face.'

'Oh yes, I suppose they could be,' I muttered, scuttling back a bit from the rail. 'Some of them might be vegetarians,' I offered lamely. After a while the fear subsided, and we marvelled at the grace of the whales, leaping out of the ocean with incredible strength. They may have been bloodthirsty, ruthless killers, but they were quite beautiful.

I woke one morning with the boat moving around rather a lot. There had been a storm some distance away during the night but, as a result, the waves had massively increased in size. Fortunately, they were travelling in the same direction that we wanted to go – only much faster than us. I stood transfixed on the afterdeck and watched as a 30ft wall of water approached. The stern rose like an elevator as the gigantic swell passed beneath us and we sank slowly into the trough. The size and power of the ocean was seriously daunting but, I told myself, this boat is made to withstand this. And it did. It went on for a day and a half and soon it didn't bother me at all. We had a couple of other incidents like one of the engines cutting out and the main cabin leaking profusely during a rainstorm, but eventually we sighted land.

It was a beautiful sunny day and, as we slowly cruised into the English Harbour, Mike and I spotted a thatched lean-to bar right on the sand. Nothing was said but within seconds we were in swimsuits, me with a £10 note clenched between my teeth, diving over the side and heading for our first cold, local beer. It's probably the best drink I've ever had.

At the quay all the boats were docked stern-to. This makes much more room than if you are tied up alongside. Also, the name and home port of the yacht is clearly displayed on the stern and you can easily run the gangplank on to the sidewalk. I noticed that there were boats from all over the world, advertising their home port next to their names. The *Braemar* had just its name, in large brass letters. They stood out about an inch from the hull and were very impressive. But no home port was mentioned.

'Ahh,' I thought. 'An opportunity for a helpful little gift.'

The next afternoon I found a shop and bought some black, plastic stick-on lettering – each about 4 inches high. That evening Mike, Wendy, Linda and I went out for dinner in a nearby restaurant. I made some excuse over the coffee and nipped back to the boat. In the middle of yachts and schooners, registered in St Tropez, Nassau, and New York, in deliberately wonky lettering, I applied the name of *Braemar's* home port … SURBITON.

Sometimes, you just have to do what seems right and proper.

I had some time off from work in the mid-1970s and Linda was opening for Elton John on one of his tours. I wanted to be with her, but not as 'a passenger' and so offered my services as a driver. I told Tony Gourvish, 'You don't need to pay me. Just get me a nice car and foot the bill for rooms in some luxurious country hotels.' He offered me the job as a tour manager and Linda and I shared her days off together.

Linda also opened for Cat Stevens on his 1974 *Bamboozle* tour. This time we put a band together for her. We recruited Gerry Conway, Cat's drummer, Phil Chen was on bass, Max Middleton on piano and I was the guitarist. This was a very prestigious world tour and to be part of it was a big deal. Cat was very generous and there were no egos on show. We would close the first half and, after an initial duet with Linda, Cat introduced her and left the stage. This was how the concerts were planned and usually went down fine, but at one concert, at the 2,000-seater Paris Olympia (a small venue compared to some of the arenas we played), the French audience didn't like it and gave us the bird. Maybe they thought Cat wasn't coming back. I don't know.

Anyhow, we finished our first song to much jeering and booing. I was incensed and addressed the crowd. 'Anyone here speak English?' Some of the crowd responded and so I yelled, 'Well, fuck off!'

We cleared the stage and didn't go back. I was so angry at their rude behaviour. They had insulted my girl. She was, after all, no slouch and certainly didn't deserve this loutish reaction. The intermission was taken early, Cat opened for the second half and we returned for the encore to a muted response.

Apart from the huge advantage of having Linda on the tour with me, I had become great friends with Alun Davies. When this world tour began in Newcastle, we had arrived a day early and, as any musician will tell you, it's the days off that really hurt. Alun and I thought it would be a good idea to have a few beers in his room after the bar closed. Room service operated for twenty-four hours and we continued to order more beer until about 8.30 a.m. when we decided to go down to breakfast. The word was out about us and, as we exited the elevator into the lobby, the front desk staff gave us a round of applause. These small moments of appreciation are what makes it all worthwhile.

Cat Stevens is a very complex man. In part because there are three versions of him: Steven Georgiou, Cat Stevens and Yusuf Islam. He's a great guy and extremely talented. The world tour I was on was promoting the *Catch Bull at Four* album. Cat, or Steve as we all called him, was in his numerology phase. As soon as he met you, he would ask your date of birth, add up the number of letters in your name and then tell you how those numerical values would affect your life path.

I realised later that he had been searching for some guiding influence all his life and that eventually led him to a serious study of

Islam. He is, in my opinion, a very committed Muslim. And although some of the rules associated with that religion are quite strict by Christian standards he has not really changed. We met more recently after a London concert and he greeted me with such warmth and kindness you wouldn't know we hadn't seen each other for about thirty years.

It's difficult to believe, but when I first met Steve, he was still somewhat of a wild boy. Capable of getting drunk and acting the fool. On one particular occasion, while in Chicago, Steve, Linda, Alun and I had been out to dinner on a night off. Drink had been taken.

'I'm feeling a bit hot,' I say. 'It would be nice to go for a swim.'

The others agreed. 'Yeah, good idea! Let's go back to the hotel and find the pool.'

As befitting a star of Steve's magnitude, we were staying downtown in some fabulous place. The pool was on the fourth floor, but it was now two o' clock in the morning and the pool was closed. Undeterred we pushed and shoved at the locked glass doors, but to no avail.

'I know,' says Steve, in a moment of blinding insight. 'Let's see what happens if I throw this chair at the doors.' Unsurprisingly, the glass splintered, leaving great shards hanging from the frame. But not enough space to climb through. Before anyone could say, 'Use the bloody chair, you wanker,' Steve was poking at the glass with his fingers, with even fewer surprising results ...

'Ouch! Sod it, I've cut myself.'

'Let's have a look,' says Alun, taking charge. 'Oh God, it's really deep.'

We crowded around to see the gash on the middle finger of his left hand. Just where the guitar strings would rest.

'Let's get you to a doctor.' We ran to reception, called the tour manager and Steve was whisked away to the emergency room. We all felt terrible. Poor Steve. A complete disaster. If he couldn't play, then the rest of the tour was in jeopardy. A nightmare. And the thing was, I was still hot.

The following afternoon at about 2 p.m., Steve called my room, explaining that he would have to take a break from playing guitar but could try to play the songs on piano. He asked if I could learn all his guitar parts by 6 p.m. for the sound check. My head said 'No', but my mouth said, 'Yes.'

Frantically I rehearsed with Alun, right up to show time. Steve went on with an enormous bandage the size of a small turban on his middle finger. Although it elicited waves of sympathy, it did absolutely nothing for his piano technique. Racked with remorse, I had learned all the notes and in the right order but couldn't emulate his style in just a few hours. The concert was pretty shabby and so the management decided to halt the tour and decamp to Arizona where the warm weather would help heal Steve's badly cut finger.

A week's holiday. Hooray! This was a five-month tour, so an enforced break was welcome. We arrived at Yuma in the middle of the night at a ranch-style hotel – maybe just a couple of steps up from a motel but with better towels. We were on the outskirts of town in the semi-desert, surrounded by huge cacti and scrub, most likely teaming with rattlesnakes. I preferred to observe the landscape from the safety of a lounger by the pool.

Tequila.

Up to this point I thought it was a drink with a dead worm in the bottom so best to be avoided. Were you supposed to eat the worm? What the hell was it doing in your drink anyway? What kind of people put invertebrates in their drink? And if this stuff kills worms what will it do to my liver? But do you know what? Down in Arizona you should do as the natives do. Margaritas, straight shots with lime and salt, and anything else containing the juice of the Blue Agave cactus. The funny thing about tequila is that when you drink anything the next morning, even a glass of water, it somehow reactivates the stuff and you get drunk all over again.

Dangerous. We were a jolly bunch on that tour.

We spent lazy days in Yuma, playing backgammon, reading, making music and lounging by the pool and making sure we were suitably refreshed. We all carried some sort of music and I had a Sony pro cassette player with a couple of battery-operated speakers. It was a surprisingly good sound. One evening we found ourselves hanging out in Cat's suite. I hesitate to call it that as it was just a couple of the adjoining rooms with the bed removed and a few more sofas added. Still it worked fine for a place to get together. Now far be it from me to confess to doing anything at all illegal but even though I obviously did not inhale, there were certain substances to be smoked.

Music, friends, tequila and grass make for a very good evening. As Keith Moon once said to me, 'I don't drink any more, but I don't drink any less either.' So, the shank of the evening appears, and we stagger off to bed. I have a vague feeling that something might be adrift. Did I leave something behind? As I fell out of my clothes and into the bed, I thought something was missing … where did I leave my guitar? Where was my wallet? Oh well, I guess I'll find out in the morning.

A couple of hours later I am woken by a strange apparition standing at the foot of the bed, dressed in canary yellow and wearing a very strange hat.

'Quick get out of bed now! Don't take anything with you. Just get out. Go to the parking lot and stand back from the building!'

Up until then I hadn't noticed that there was an awful lot of noise. Coming from the ringing of bells it seems. Linda and I managed to find our way out and joined the crowd. There were firemen all over the place, sirens blaring and someone being assertive with a bullhorn. Nasty.

'We must have been really out of it to not hear the fire alarm,' I murmured above the racket.

'Anyone know what's going on?'

'There's a fire in Steve's suite and they only just got him out in time.'

'It's lucky we were all on the ground floor!'

'Yeah, anyone know how it started?'

REMEMBER … Never ask a question if you don't want to hear the answer.

'The firemen think it started in the sofa. Apparently, a cigarette was dropped down there. It took a while to get going, but when it did, the whole room went up.'

Oh shit. I remember now. The end fell off that joint and slipped between the seat cushions. I managed to get the burning end part back on to the joint but possibly a tiny itzy bitzy, minuscule, pathetically small ember might possibly, unknowingly, accidentally, unhappily, just on this one occasion, remained.

Thank God no one asked me if I knew anything.

We skipped town the next day.

It was during this tour that I met one of my rivals for Linda's affections. It was Muhammad Ali. We had been staying in a hotel in New Zealand and Linda and I had had a row and I had gone for a walk. Linda had noticed him in the lobby of the hotel – I suppose he wasn't easy to miss. Handsome, charismatic and still a powerful figure. A little later and also a little more tipsy, Linda had staggered upstairs to what she thought was our room. It was, in fact, Ali's suite and he was, according to Linda, surrounded by an entourage of stunning girls.

Ali invited Linda in and started chatting her up at which point I had returned to the hotel and hearing some noise in the next room, found her sitting next to the Champ.

'And who is that?' Ali asked Linda.

She reluctantly replied, 'That's my husband.'

'Yes, I am,' I added helpfully.

Ali turned to Linda and asked, 'What you doing with that honky?'

I could easily have been angered by this remark and considered my actions. I could either bob and weave, lead with my left and finish him off with an uppercut – or apologise for indeed being white. Ali then smiled disarmingly. He was joking. Thank goodness for that.

It was just good-natured banter. The Louisville Lip was joshing. We chatted for a while and Ali was charming and extremely funny.

Of course, I've often wondered what might have happened had the encounter turned nasty. I reckon I could have handled myself against the greatest ever heavyweight champion of the world. I could have been a contender. All I needed was to sting like a butterfly and float like a bee.

Or something like that ...

'Age', 'Plum' and us three 'Eejits'.

My first London band, The Coronado Four, in Portscatho, Cornwall. Left to right: Ken Mckay, Yours truly, Pete Hocking and Adrian Sumption.

Blossom Toes –
Psychedelia's Lonely
Hearts Club Band.
Left to right: Me,
Brian Godding, Brian
Belshaw, Kevin Westlake.
*(Pictorial Press Ltd/
Alamy Stock Photo)*

Linda, me and Mick – 'Remember the Days'.

'Even the Sex Police feared a knock on the door from the Sex Police.' Left to right: Rod, me, Robin Le Mesurier, Malcolm Cullimore.

Elton taking the pith in Sun City.

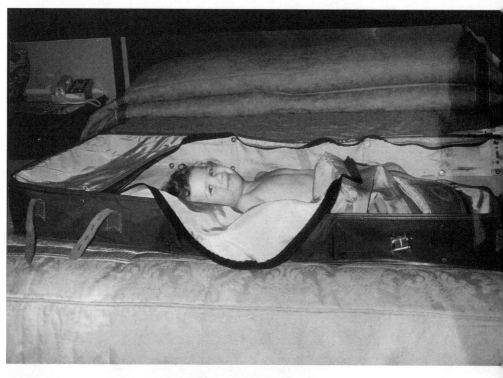

Camille putting it on at the Ritz, Palm Beach.

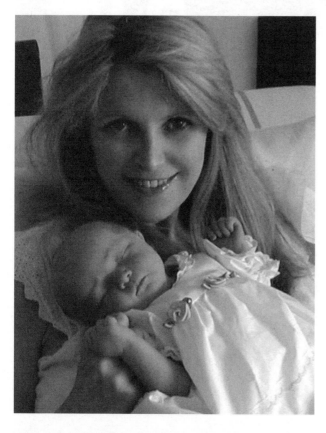

Mandy and baby Ava.

Mackenzie, guitar slinger. *(Matthew Fleming)*

The beautiful, witty and gracious Camille. *(Brian Braff)*

Camille's wedding. The happiest of days in Tuscany. *(Monica Leggio)*

4

Far, Far from Ferraris

If Rod Stewart was playing in my back garden, I wouldn't bother to open the curtains.

Some Bloke in a Bar

After Family split up in 1974, I was offered a job with Bad Company, but I no longer wanted to play bass and instead joined Cockney Rebel, following a recommendation from their bass player, George Ford. Rumours abounded that Steve Harley was a pain in the arse, somewhat arrogant and difficult. But he wasn't. We worked together at one recording session at Air London and we got on just fine. Then, out of the blue, Steve rang and asked if I would like to play the Reading Festival. I agreed, thinking I would be employed for just this one gig.

This one gig was something special. The audience amounted to 35,000 people and I'd only had two days of rehearsals. Halfway through the one-hour set, the wind blew all my notes and chord sheets across the stage and away forever. Bloody scary. I didn't know the songs very well and, to this day, don't know how I got through it.

Steve is a fantastic front man. I was astounded by his stage presence and how easily he won the love of the audience. He had been struck down with polio when he was a child and had spent years in hospital, undergoing a couple of major surgeries. Because of his disability in one leg, he couldn't dance or go down on his knees, but had been a champion swimmer and so his upper body was very developed. He had very large hands, which he used to convey emotion. When he put them alongside his face, palms outwards to the audience, he had a Marcel Marceau quality. It was stylised, but incredibly effective. He is an extraordinary live performer.

Immediately after the show, he asked me to join the band. I was up for it, although some of my serious musician friends were surprised I was joining what was considered a pop band. The decision to be part of Cockney Rebel was quickly rewarded when the first record with the band made number one in the album and single charts.

Pink Floyd's engineer Alan Parsons produced the first album that I played on and we recorded it at Abbey Road. I'd never heard 'Make Me Smile (Come Up and See Me)' before we went into the studio, but my guitar break made some waves. I didn't even know that I was going to do an acoustic solo. It was about one o'clock in the morning and we'd had a few drinks. There were just two takes, which were spliced together. I didn't even think it was going to sound that good – the band were pleased but not exactly overcome with admiration. We all went home after that and it was only in the weeks, months and years to come that the solo became so iconic. One radio DJ on Radio 1 took the needle off the record and played my break again. Eric Clapton actually congratulated me and, in a momentary lapse of judgement, later named me as one of his favourite guitarists.

Steve was always one for making an impression. The climax of this British tour was to play an open-air festival at Crystal Palace. Each of us was provided with a limousine to take us there so we would arrive in style – and in convoy. A fleet of Austin Princesses. Steve had planned to have underwater fireworks in the lake and exploding jets of water shooting into the air and to top it all, a wooden platform had been built just 6 inches under the surface of the water. We had also installed a quadraphonic sound system, which only us, as the 'headliners', were allowed to use. This was the forerunner of surround sound. The sound mixer had a little joystick, which if utilised correctly, could send the notes of all the instruments whizzing around the park. Unfortunately, earlier in the day, the mixer had developed a fault, so the quadraphonic sound was untested. We took to the stage straight after Steeleye Span, who had rocked the joint spectacularly. A tough act to follow at the best of times.

The first moment of impending doom was when Stuart Elliott hit the first snare drum beat. The extra speakers at the back of the park were so loud the echo of the snare was louder than the original sound coming off the stage. The sound engineers had not taken into account the natural time delay between the sound on stage and the return. We could hear ourselves completely out of time – not knowing which beat to follow. Somehow, we managed to play through this cacophony for a couple of songs.

Then the crowd surged forward. It was a beautiful day. People were hot. The lake in front of the stage was enticing. They jumped in. They swam. They discovered the platform that was placed for Steve to do his walking on water act. They leapt upon it and ran straight on the stage to dance and party with us. Total chaos. Steve tried to warn them about the danger from the hidden explosives in the lake, but this warning went unheeded in the excitement. Thank goodness none of the fireworks went off.

We played on despite the chaos. The audience were soaked through and with all plans for the pyrotechnic effects abandoned, we left the stage dejected. Not only had all Steve's grandiose planning come to nothing, Steeleye Span were better than us! We slunk home in our separate limos, sobbing silently into the night.

We were about to start our first US tour as a support act to the Kinks. Steve needed to stay behind for some nebulous reason and the band went to LA ahead of him a couple of days earlier. Keyboard wiz Duncan Mackay had found a fake broken arm plaster cast which he decided I should wear to greet Steve on his arrival. So, we were gathered at the pool at the Sunset Marquis Hotel as Steve arrived. I was at the far end, wearing the cast, and waved at him with my free arm.

'Hi Steve, welcome to LA.'

Steve was horrified. 'Jim, what the hell? This is a disaster. How did that happen?'

'It's only a scratch. I'll be OK in a few weeks and I'm not too bad with my right hand. Don't worry, it will be OK.'

'What are you talking about? This is a disaster.' Steve slumped into a nearby lounger.

Drummer Stuart Elliot was dismissive. 'Oh, Jim, you're such a drama queen.' And promptly shoved me into the pool.

The last thing I hear before I hit the water was Steve shouting, 'Noooo … watch out for his good arm.' His face was a picture when I climbed out the pool without the cast and completed my annual push-up.

We had reached number one in the single and album charts, and so we travelled pretty well. We flew on scheduled airlines and would be met on the tarmac by pre-arranged transport. We always had a van for the luggage and a limousine for the band. In contrast, Ray Davies and the Kinks had a greyhound bus that would meet them, and we were vaguely embarrassed that the star was riding in these shabby buses and we were swanning around and being a bit flash in our limo. After a week or so, Steve decided we should get a minibus, so as not to outdo Ray, but on that very same day, Ray hired a couple of limos. The highly charged look on his face, when he discovered this, was wonderful – as if we had set him up. I thought he might break into an emotional version of 'You Really Got Me' there and then.

Ray was quite mercurial, which made approaching him occasionally difficult. However, the girl singers in his band were great fun and wanted to come out to play with us. We were so successful at entertaining them that Ray tried to ban them from spending any time with us. Needless to say, no one took any notice and it was a very happy tour for the rest of us. There was only one major hiccup, when, one night, our equipment van broke down. Without our instruments we informed the promoter that we couldn't go on.

'That's all right,' he said, smiling sweetly. 'It's up to you, but if you don't go on, I'll break your legs.' And if he meant the whole band that would be a lot of legs. Somehow, we managed to borrow some gear, played a blinder and received a couple of encores. It turned out to be one of our better shows on that tour. Fear is a great motivator.

It was on this tour that I first played at the legendary Whisky a Go Go club on Sunset Strip. It was quite something to perform at the club that had witnessed the birth of the Los Angeles rock scene and hosted the Doors, Janis Joplin and Zeppelin among many others. The only trouble with playing these renowned clubs was that the staff at the venues sometimes considered themselves more important than the bands that were playing there. They could be arrogant, patronising, and unhelpful. And that's when they were being nice. And we knew that challenging them directly might result in the odd 'accidental' technical mishap. I also remember that the microphones at the Whisky were so old, they stank of generations of the performers' breath and spittle.

We stayed at the nearby Hyatt House Hotel known as 'The Riot House', which was as mad a place to hang out as you had ever seen; groupies stalked the rooms, while trying not to get mown down by the motorbikes being raced around the corridors. Many television sets were flung from bedrooms, Jim Morrison was evicted when he hung out of his bedroom window by his fingertips and probably for other foolish behaviour and Little Richard lived – or should I say 'partied' – there during the 1980s and '90s. I recall a notice behind the reception desk which read, 'That scruffy, unwashed person standing in front of you may have enough money to buy the hotel and have you fired. Be nice.'

One night the band was playing at another fabled club in Los Angeles – the Roxy. Rod Stewart and his beautiful girlfriend Britt Ekland dropped in to the gig. I must have done something right that night because he asked Pete Buckland, his tour manager, to get my number. Sometime later, back in England, Rod asked me to meet him in a pub in Highgate. He arrived in a lime green Lamborghini Miura, still wearing his football kit. I was in a Mini Clubman estate. We got on really well and there was talk of me joining the band. But I didn't hear any more from him and figured that, maybe, I should have bought more than one round. Still, he gave me his home number in LA.

Fast forward a few months to the autumn of 1976, I was in LA playing on a session for Linda Lewis produced by Cat Stevens, so with my guitar parts finished and a couple of days off, I decided to give him a call. Britt answered – and to be honest, I would have been quite happy chatting to her for as long as she wanted, but eventually she put Rod on the line.

He told me that the band were rehearsing that very afternoon and asked me if I'd like to come down. I already knew bassist Phil Chen from the Linda Lewis Band and I had played with ex-Vanilla Fudge drummer Carmine Appice in London at the Palladium. We jammed for half an hour after which Rod asked, 'Will you learn "Maggie May" and "You Wear It Well" and come back tomorrow?'

'Of course,' I said, absolutely knocked out that this might be really happening.

I learned those tunes and a few others and returned the following day.

After an hour or so Rod called a break. He came over and putting an arm round my shoulder asked if I would like to join the band.

'Why not?' I replied, grinning from ear to ear.

And so, a friendship began that, after more than forty years, is still going strong.

But I had problem. I was still officially in Cockney Rebel and I had to let Steve Harley know that he was 'letting me go'. I returned to England and arranged to meet Steve at Kenwood House, the seventeenth-century former stately home, in Hampstead Heath. I told him I was really sorry, but that I had to leave Rebel. Steve was upset, as was I. But I felt I didn't have much choice. Rod was a huge star and wanted to include me in the songwriting. He was also offering me a percentage of the profits. Two things that I didn't have with Steve. He was based in LA and I would have to spend much time rehearsing and recording there. I had no idea just how long I would be with Rod – it might last a year or two …

And before I embarked on my adventures with Rod, stateside, there was something else I had to do. Get married. Linda and I decided to make our relationship legal. It seemed the right thing to do. There was much to arrange – including a stag do …

The party was to be held at the Knightsbridge Holiday Inn. I rented a suite at the hotel, cleared out some of the furniture and arranged for a pool table to be delivered. I organised a bar area and hired a barman. There were about thirty people invited, including members of Stud, Cockney Rebel, and family members, including brother-in-law Robert, and my brother, Maurice. When Maurice arrived, he tossed his car keys to a man in uniform, sporting a peaked cap and politely requested, 'Please park my car.' The man smiled back but said he couldn't help.

'I don't park cars, sonny, I fly aeroplanes.' Turned out the chap was a Pan Am pilot.

I knew there was going to be trouble when some members of Family arrived wearing boiler suits. The waiter brought in trays of sandwiches, which were sent flying, resulting in egg mayonnaise and coronation chicken decorating the walls. After desecrating the suite, we moved downstairs as the confines of the room were cramping our style and we needed more space. We discovered the swimming pool, bordered by a rockery. This was too tempting, and so, of course, we had to climb up on to the rockery and jump into the pool. We then believed we should all hold hands, create a huge 'bomb' and jump in.

The problem was that the rockery was 6ft wider than the pool and mayhem ensued, after which the manager approached us and told us we had to stop this nonsense. He ended up in the pool. Taking it in good humour, he joined the party and became so inebriated that he ended waking up the next morning in the same bed as brother-in-law, Robert, who happened to be wearing a black plastic mac. Robert can't remember anything about the manager or the mackintosh. He does maintain, however, that a grand piano was also launched into the pool, but we would never have done such a thing. It would have been going too far.

Unfortunately, during the shenanigans, I did have a falling out with my best man, photographer and bath tub singer, Tony Rowland. He went to the hotel receptionist and explained that I needed £350 in cash, and that this amount should be added to my bill. In fact, Tony pocketed the cash there and then. When I checked the bill, a few days later, I was bit taken aback. It was pretty horrendous what with the drinks, the food, general damages, redecoration costs, alpine plant replacements from the rockery – not to mention the actual rocks – and £350 cash. When I confronted Tony about this, he made no excuse, declaring that being so rich I wouldn't even notice. I did. I wasn't. And I haven't seen him since.

My wedding to Linda the following day was slightly more sedate. We were married in a picturesque church in East Molesey, Surrey, with the reception at a nearby restaurant in Hampton Court, which was chosen for its lack of rockery and swimming pool.

Linda looked lovely in a full-length antique lace dress. We had about eighty friends and family attend the ceremony, which was followed by a disco. We spent the night in a beautiful Elizabethan hotel near the airport in a honeymoon suite and four-poster bed. We'd been living together for five years but were both so happy that we were getting married.

Our honeymoon was spent in the Seychelles at a very luxurious hotel on Mahe, the largest island. It was the most beautiful of places, but after a couple of days, we had become a little unsettled. It was all a bit formal and the upmarket guests, although very polite, were not very exciting. One day we walked along the beach and perched on a promontory was a ramshackle hotel, the White Hall, a single storey building, with walkways and colonial atmosphere. There was a great restaurant and someone was playing jazz standards on the piano. It was much more authentic, casual and characterful than our hotel. The clientele was friendlier and lots of locals, who used the hotel as a hang-out, invited us back to their homes in the hills. We regretted that we weren't staying at the White Hall, but we still had a wonderful time.

One day, we rented a jeep and driving back from a restaurant to our hotel, in the middle of nowhere, Linda opened her handbag and threw her purse, followed by a bracelet and other items of jewellery into the jungle, announcing, 'I don't really need any of this.'

I yelled at her, 'What the hell are you doing? Stop!'

She wouldn't. A sudden desire to divest herself of her worldly treasures had engulfed her.

'Please stop,' I pleaded. 'At least, keep your engagement ring and your watch!'

Linda agreed to this request, but her shoes and further adornments went flying into the undergrowth. I had no idea what was happening. The next day, we drove back through the jungle to try and find some of her belongings, but to no avail. Later on, during the holiday, I heard that a lemur was arrested trying to sell a diamond bracelet.

My first tour with Rod began in December 1976, following the release of his solo album *Night on the Town*. He wanted to put together a predominantly British band and to create a relaxed atmosphere both off and on stage. He wrote about the tour in his autobiography, *Rod*, with particular reference to our stage gear:

I encouraged everyone to go in for flamboyance and colour. This wouldn't always work … Phil Chen would have some good little outfits, but Jim and Kevin (Savigar) would make some truly awe-inspiring mistakes and Carmine (Appice) was probably the worst of the lot; terrible snakeskin-look shirts and silver waistcoats and leather jerkins. Billy (Peek), meanwhile, was short and dumpy, and we never knew quite what to do with him, in terms of stage presentation. So, we used to dress him up as a Frenchman and leave it at that.

I feel I have a right to reply. Before the opening night of a tour there would be a fashion show, which would take place in the hotel's corridor. We would always reserve a whole corridor for the band and roadies etc. and usually occupy the rooms in the same order, so we knew who the next-door neighbours were. The bedroom doors were always left open as we were in and out of each other's rooms.

We would try on our new stage outfits and then meet in the corridor and see what everyone thought. We had all laid out some serious money for our gear. The more flamboyant amongst us (yours truly) would never buy off the peg. I have to say I adopted some dreadful costumes. Sometimes, I looked as stylish as a bull in a tutu.

It was a nerve-racking experience. I soon discovered that you had to be willing to take a punch. There was much piss taking, but it was mainly good natured in a spirit of camaraderie. Rod was always being ridiculed about his nose, skinny legs and he too had to grin and bear it. At one point, he appeared in a makeshift Arab outfit, complete with fez in a sort Hollywood notion of Bedouin costume. He resembled Douglas Fairbanks in *The Thief of Baghdad*. Of course, the band fell about laughing and the regalia was never seen again. Rod donned in a 'matador suit of lights', which was all twinkly in black and gold. He looked very self-conscious and before anyone could quip, 'The bull went thataway' to 'Hello, this must be the Toro tour', Rod muttered, 'I think I've made a mistake,' before adding brightly, 'But, Jim, it would look good on you.'

Some of my outfits were also disastrous; I had seen a suede jacket where the sleeves were gathered into folds, which hung from my arms and grew larger towards my hands. I thought it looked great and had a similar woollen suit made. Unfortunately, the result was that I looked exactly like the Michelin man, but with the air let out. Deflated in every sense, I wore it for a lifetime total of a minute and half.

Billy Peek was the third guitarist, but not involved in every song. He would take to the stage and specifically play rock and roll. In fact, everything I learned about playing rock and roll I learned from Billy. One fantastic tip, which turned out to be paramount when playing rhythm guitar, was that your right hand should be all even down-strokes – like playing a high hat. All the accents and feel comes from the left-hand damping and releasing the strings.

I later imparted this wisdom to Will Sexton, a singer-songwriter, whose album I was producing. His reaction was, 'Is that it? That's the most important thing you ever learned?' I shrugged, vaguely disappointed that he hadn't grasped the importance of the concept. Fast forward five years. Will calls me at home, 'Hey, Jim, that thing you showed me. I get it. It's amazing. Thanks.' Shame it took him so long, but he did get there in the end.

Those were halcyon days. I was doing well and Linda was making some money from her records, when Alun Davies suggested we move from our flat to be near him in Surrey. We thus acquired a two-up, two-down cottage in East Molesey. At the bottom of the garden ran the River Mole and so we bought a boat, which we named *Duck Soup*. I'd always dreamed of having a home by some water and here I was, enjoying the most fun I could have with a small boat on a river. I could cast off and drift downstream. The Mole flowed into the Thames to a pub called the Swan, which became one of my locals. Late, one night, when my parents were staying, I suggested to my dad that we go out in the boat. I had a bottle of brandy and Age had a bottle of whisky. We stayed up all night chatting and about 5 a.m.,

I switched off the engine and drifted down under the morning sky for what seemed like an eternity. Much peaceful imbibing and the only commotion came from a few disgruntled fishermen who cursed us for disturbing their sport. That sojourn with my father was one of my favourite memories of my time with him.

My accountant then advised us that we needed to invest some money, and property seemed the best thing. So, we moved from East Molesey and bought a house in Oxshott, on a private road just 5 miles away. I missed the river, but we had much more space, extensive grounds and five bedrooms – rock star bollocks. I bought a flash sportscar, which elicited a response from my Aunt Rita, ''Tis far, far from Ferraris that you were raised.' In retrospect, it was a shame, in a way, to get caught up in this flamboyant lifestyle, but there seemed to be a certain inevitability about it. I was still quite young, but I can't blame everything on my youth. There must be part of my personality that enjoyed that way of living … and I loved fast cars. Still do.

Rod and some of the band were based in Los Angeles and so, for work purposes, I moved temporarily across the pond to the City of Angels – there's a misnomer, if ever I heard one. With other members of the band, I was holed up at the Beverly Hilton or L'Hermitage. I suppose 'holed up' is another inaccurate term – both were very luxurious hotels and we were looked after very well in these establishments. Linda remained in the UK as she was still working but would visit when she could. This lovely lifestyle could and should have lasted for longer, but for Carmine Appice.

The drummer had a lovely six-bedroom house in Los Feliz near the Greek Amphitheatre and Griffith Park. He reckoned that we didn't need hotel accommodation and so suggested to Rod that we move to furnished apartments, which would be cheaper than the hotels. I'd like to be charitable to Carmine and think that he might have been doing us a favour – there were tennis courts and a swimming pool and hotel life can be transitory. But the other point was that the band worked as a co-operative and we shared the profits of touring – and the apartments would be less expensive.

Unfortunately, we ended up in in the Oakwood apartments, which turned out to be very seedy. The swimming pool appeared to be a health hazard due to the colour of the water and the indescribable objects floating in the shallow end. It was a very dismal block and the accommodation was depressing; dark, gloomy, stained carpets, shabby furniture. The outlook, directly across from my living room, was into the ground floor of a three-storey concrete parking structure.

I was very grumpy with Carmine, as were all the band members who weren't resident in the USA and needed temporary accommodation. I've always been very aware of my surroundings. It doesn't have to be expensive or glamorous, but I need to be able to see the sky, some trees and maybe some water. I'd lived in much worse places in London, but nothing as quite as dark and oppressive as the Oakwood apartments. I wondered what the fuck I was doing when I had a beautiful house and garden back home and although my relationship with Linda was difficult at times, I was also missing her and I became quite depressed.

Up until then, Linda had been very successful career-wise and, in her prime, certainly enjoyed and made the most of her fame. At one stage she was happy to ride her bicycle locally, but when she became more famous, she gave up the two-wheel mode of transport and would only travel by car – even regularly hiring a limo from our house in Oxshott to do a little shopping at Harrods! Unfortunately, coming to terms with her success was difficult for her in other ways. As time passed, the stress of performing had become increasingly anxiety provoking and resulted in her having to resort to medication to get through.

On one occasion, Linda headlined the Festival Hall, fronting a fifteen-piece band and string section. But before the concert, she lost her nerve and she locked herself in the toilet, refusing to leave. We all tried to persuade her to come out, without success, until her manager stood outside and, within earshot, called out, 'OK. Linda's not going on. Does anyone have Shirley Bassey's number?' Linda shot out of the toilet as if fired by a canon – I suppose you could say this bluff 'flushed' her out. Anyway, Linda gathered herself, took to the stage and was absolutely fantastic.

Clive Davis is a former lawyer and record executive who was president of Columbia Records before founding Arista records. He signed Linda to the label, and in 1975 album her album *Not A Little Girl Anymore* was released. Clive was huge in the business and would work very hard for his artists – as long as they agreed to everything he suggested.

Linda was booked to play at Carnegie Hall in New York – an incredibly prestigious concert to celebrate the first anniversary of Arista Records. Although I wasn't playing, I escorted her to the event. She wasn't well that night, suffering with a flu bug, but being a proper trouper, she managed to perform brilliantly at the concert and proved to be a huge success with the audience. We returned to the hotel to change before the reception, but Linda was just too ill to attend the party. She rang Clive Davis and left a message to that effect. He never returned her call and despite her trying to contact him on a number of occasions, Linda didn't hear from him ever again. Clive Davis never released any more of her records and, in my opinion, this was the beginning of the end of her career.

Linda's own family background had been pretty unstable and had no doubt affected her. She was also devastated that we couldn't have children. After about a year of us trying, she visited a psychic, and recorded her interview with him. Without any prompting, he told her, 'You're having trouble conceiving a child. You will have an operation to clear your fallopian tubes in July of this year.' Linda was amazed he knew any of this; however, he had the wrong date. The operation was scheduled for October, not July. He also told her, 'You have a red car. It's unlucky, you need to get rid of it.' We had three cars at that time: my red Dino Ferrari 246, a chocolate brown Mercedes 300 SE convertible and an orange Mini Clubman estate we used as a run-around.

Soon after, Rod had suggested we should borrow his house for a holiday in Estepona, a resort town on Spain's Costa del Sol. He and Britt had broken up and he was now with Alana, the ex-wife of actor George Hamilton. Rod's place was a six-bedroomed house right next to the sea, complete with tennis court. Linda and I thought we were going to be there on our own, but Rod and Alana arrived unexpectedly. What a great surprise! Along with Pete Buckland and actress Leslie Ash, we were a dangerous crew.

I had driven there in the Ferrari and Rod had that lime green Lamborghini Miura. We would race along the coast highway, in what we called 'The Estepona Grand Prix'. We'd hurtle around bends at over 100mph. I guess I must have learned a thing or two from my few days training at Brand's Hatch motor racing school but how we didn't end up in jail or hospital I'll never know.

It was a great trip, but on the way home, Linda complained of severe abdominal pains, which had become so unbearable that on the drive back from Dover, we had to stop in A&E in Reigate and were advised to see Ian Craft, an obstetric consultant at the Royal Free Hospital urgently. We saw him the following day, Linda had an ectopic pregnancy and he operated on her straightaway. The operation had taken place in July as predicted by the psychic.

Six months later, Linda fell asleep at the wheel, ploughed into a parked car and, not wearing a seat belt, was thrown through the windscreen. Her front teeth shattered and went through her lip. Thankfully she recovered OK.

The official name for the colour of her car – the little orange Mini Clubman estate – was Fiesta red. It was inexplicable how the psychic's prophesies had come true and although I can be sceptical about the paranormal, I have no doubt that there are forces at work that we don't understand. Most of them being record executives.

Having said that, despite all this evidence and the psychic's warnings, I certainly wasn't going to get rid of my red Ferrari.

My first album with Rod and the band was *Foot Loose & Fancy Free*, and this was followed by a North American tour. I was away for a couple of months, our last gig taking place in Daly City in December 1977 before we returned to London. It was quite a tour and some foolish behaviour that was to become part of our Spinal Tap impressions had already begun to happen.

Rod referred to our flight home from Los Angeles in his autobiography:

> The realisation was dawning on me that this time we had gone too far. Certainly, the sight of Jim Cregan, my guitarist, his curly hair full of ash and cigarette butts, and his face smeared with what seemed, upon closer inspection, to be honey, would have been a decent clue ... behind us lay British Airways first-class cabin liberally re-decorated with mustard. And ahead of us lay a rightful bashing in the press for our disgraceful behaviour.

Mainly true, I'm afraid. I had made the mistake on that particular flight of falling asleep and so had to be punished for an earlier discretion mid-air. While Rod had been occupied elsewhere, I purloined his cowboy boots and emptied a jar of mustard and a couple of bags of peanuts into them and then proceeded to mix the ingredients thoroughly. When I woke to discover my face smeared with honey and witness the fruits of my sabotage, I was both dismayed and full of admiration. For on leaving the plane, Rod donned his boots without a murmur and exited the plane without a hint of acknowledgement of the horrors within his footwear. One of the things I love about Rod is that he believed in the maxim, 'If you are going to dish it out you also have to be able to take it.' He didn't get preferential treatment and was prepared to put up with reasonable retaliation at all times. And it didn't seem fair that as a result of the band's on-board behaviour, it was Rod and not the rest of us who was subsequently banned by British Airways. We had the whole of the first-class cabin apart from a few other passengers who understandably complained about us and, feeling a little guilty, we paid their fares, so they ended up with a free passage to blighty. It was the least we could do …

The *Blondes Have More Fun* tour, a couple of years later began in Paris and ended in Los Angeles. For the last night of the run of shows at the LA Forum, Rod agreed to rent a London bus, equipped with a bar, which was to transport us from the gig to the party afterwards. The double-decker was packed with girlfriends, wives, family and friends, all in high spirits, mainly garnered from the bar. Rod and Alana were sitting across the aisle from me when something happened to upset her. The next thing I knew was that she was storming to the back of the bus and as the traffic paused, she jumped off the platform and into the street. Before anyone could do anything, the bus pulled away from the lights, leaving her stranded. We didn't realise that we were in Inglewood, South Central LA, a neighbourhood not known for its warm welcome to visiting socialites – especially a glamorous blonde, dressed in just a skimpy, short dress. Fortunately, a passing police cruiser soon picked her up. Considering the mood that Alana was in, they were probably pleased that they were able to put her in a partitioned area in the back of the car. The motto of the Los Angeles police force is 'To Protect and to Serve'. I reckon that night they needed protection from Alana rather than the other way around.

5

Hollywood and Bust

You know, you're really nobody in LA unless you live in a house with a really big door.

Steve Martin

By the end of the decade my relationship with Linda was pretty volatile. We had separated more than once but had somehow survived and were still together. We thought that a permanent move to the States might be good for us and in 1980, I started looking for houses in Los Angeles. On the advice of my accountant, we decided to sell the house in Oxshott. Now, looking back, it was terrible advice. Although we would have been liable for more tax, the house would be worth a small fortune now. Anyhow, the actor Anthony Valentine made us an offer, which was less than others we received, but we liked him a lot and wanted the house to be a home to someone we were keen on.

Being the financial genius that I am today, we put the profits in pound sterling in my British bank. This process took about three months during which time the pound was devalued heavily against the dollar taking a large bite out of the deposit. If only I had put the money in my American bank … What a mug! But I did I find the perfect house on Fareholm Drive in the Hollywood Hills. It sat on a bluff at the entrance to Laurel Canyon with a spectacular uninterrupted view across the city. It was a two-storey building in the Cape Cod style with a shaded balcony running across the whole length of the house accessed by French windows from the master and guest bedrooms. It had a total of four bedrooms and a separate guest house. We loved it and settled into a new life.

The new life inevitably involved much partying. Although Rod had broken up with Britt Ekland, we had remained friendly with her. One evening, after a show at the Troubadour, we found ourselves at Britt's house in Stone Canyon and I ended up sat next to Keith Richards. On a coffee table in front of us, he measured out the longest line of coke I had ever seen – about a foot in length.

'Oh good,' I thought, 'this will be nice,' whereupon Keith proceeded to snort the whole lot. Thanks very much, Keith. It's incredible that despite all the abuse, being electrocuted, falling out of coconut trees and various health risks, Keith is still going strong and remains so creative. I think he is the greatest rock riff writer that we have ever had. Tunes like 'Brown Sugar', 'Satisfaction', 'Honky Tonk Women' and many others all have iconic, memorable hard-rocking riffs.

Keith was on *Desert Island Discs* a couple of years ago and the presenter, Kirsty Young, asked him if rock and roll was a seemly place for someone in their 70s to be. After a slight pause and with that wonderfully infectious chuckle, Keith replied, 'I've never worried about being seemly. I'm here and I rock and roll.' A perfect response. Thanks, Keith, on behalf of all of us aging rock and rollers …

So I was making records. The session fees were pretty good, and I was also receiving songwriting royalties. There was a spare shilling around, so we decided to completely refurbish and redecorate the place. We employed a local guy and his team and work began. I have to say they took to their labour with a vigour and earnestness that I hadn't expected. There was also much chatter between them. I was delighted that they were happy in their work.

One afternoon, needing to speak to the crew during their lunch break, I went outside to have a word with them. I walked, unseen, to the side door of their van and heard a lot of snorting and sniffing. Oh dear, I thought they must have all got colds – or maybe developed allergies to some of the building materials. Perhaps, they'd been imbibing too much coffee. I looked in the window and saw them all hunched over album covers with rolled up $20 bills protruding from their schnozzles. Ahhh … you know you're in LA when the builders are snorting coke.

My parents, initially upset that I had moved across the pond, understood my reasons and visited most winters from then on. When the building work on the house was nearly completed, I invited Plum and Age, as well as my brother Maurice and his wife Judy to come and stay. The place was pretty well finished except for the swimming pool. Now, just a note about swimming pool builders. They tell you they can start in a couple of days. This sounds great. So, they come in with a digger and then rip an enormous hole in the garden. They then disappear for three or four months, having fulfilled their contractual obligation to start on time. Bastards.

Despite that, we were having a great time as a family with lots of dinners and occasional imprudent behaviour. There was a massive hedge bordering the property to the south which needed cutting back as it blocked our spectacular view, looking out across the city.

Maurice suggested we do the work ourselves. 'How hard can it be? You've got this enormous hedge trimmer, let's have a go.'

The house and garden were gouged into the side of the hill at the entrance to Laurel Canyon. The hedge grew up from the street below and was about 15ft high. It was also about 15ft deep by the time it reached up to the garden but was quite easy to lean into about 6ft of it. I suggested Maurice should crawl across the top of the hedge to finish the job.

'Bugger off!' came the immediate and unequivocal reply. 'Let's tie the trimmer to a pole to give us the extra reach.'

'Good idea!'

So, we chucked the trimmer on to the top of the hedge and dragged it around holding the broom-handle until we got bored and tired. I can't remember which came first. The result looked like it had been attacked by a swarm of airborne great white sharks.

But the view ...

Late one afternoon, about the time the British pubs would have opened, a thirst came upon us. Age, Maurice and I told the girls, who were preparing a fine roast dinner, that a swift half was needed and we would be back soon. We zoomed down the hill to La Cienega Boulevard and the Coronet pub. Of course, this is not a real pub, but it was a local bar and the owner, Nick, was a fine chap. So we settled at the bar and began to put the world to rights. (Despite having put the world to rights on several occasions I am always amazed how it invariably remains exactly the same – even after all my application and exertion.)

Now, across the street from the pub is a strip club and the girls would invariably come in and have a drink before or after work. As we frequented the place quite regularly, we got to know them a little bit. On this occasion, several of them wanted to meet Age. I don't know what it was about him; maybe because he looked a bit like a cross between Sir John Gielgud and Dame Margaret Rutherford, or because they mistakenly thought he was a harmless old bloke, but the strippers loved him.

'Age, how long is it since you have been in a strip club?' one of them asks, fluttering her cleavage and flashing her eyelashes. Anyway, Age appears indignant.

'Oh I've never been in one at all,' he lies, getting a tiny bit hot around his Van Heusen collar.

'Me neither,' says Maurice.

'Well, you boys had better come and see, we're on in a few minutes.'

Before you could say 'Gypsy Rose Lee', we pay Nick and weave our way across six lanes of traffic and into the club. One of the things you have to get used to in LA is the shock of leaving very glaring bright sunlight and entering a darkened room. You immediately think you've gone blind. Being a very shy and retiring little group, we choose to sit at the back on a banquette with a fixed drinks table in front of us. Watered down versions of vodka and tonic were placed in front of us and we settled back for the show.

Well, we have been there no longer than twenty minutes when we hear a loud commotion at the front door and some raised voices.

'I know they're in here, their car is parked outside the pub. No! We are not paying any admission, we're just coming to take them away.'

Oh God! The fun police are here.

Judy and Linda storm in, searching about in the gloom before their eyes have adjusted. The show is now no longer on the stage but right here. Our immediate thought was to put our hands up, admit defeat and slump away with our wives. So, the three of us slide down under the table as far as we can in a pathetic attempt to hide. Unfortunately, the giveaway is Maurice's omnipresent Panama hat sitting on the table.

'We're buggered,' I whisper to the lads as the wives reach our table. 'And we're trapped,' I added somewhat needlessly.

'Ahh caught you, you ratbags! You worthless wretches! Sit up and look at me,' says Judy, eyes blazing. 'The dinner is ruined and here you are in this dreadful place.' With that, she takes a huge swing at Maurice's head with her handbag. Of course, he ducked. Next in line was Age. He ducked. And I ducked.

The ferocious momentum carried the bag all the way round to Linda who was right next to Judy. Whack! It caught Linda in the chest and she staggered back clutching at the table as she went but only grabbing the Panama and collapsing in a heap. The club erupted with laughter – even the strippers giving the girls a round of applause and to their credit the wives saw the funny side of it.

We all left with no further bloodshed.

The dinner was still delicious.

But Maurice never got his hat back.

***

Well, we added a jacuzzi with views of the city and we did get the swimming pool finished, which Linda was very excited about. She should have been, as it cost $28,000, which in today's money is about $82,000. Unfortunately, this was about the only thing we could get excited about, as the marriage was on the rocks and we realised that we just couldn't continue living together. Linda's behaviour had become erratic, I was unhappy and we had both been unfaithful. I had managed only two swims in the pool, which, by my reckoning, works out at $14,000 a dip ($41,000 today) before I moved out, renting a house in Cresthill Road, in the nearby Hollywood Hills, next door to Twiggy and just around the corner from Roger Taylor, Queen's drummer. Linda and I had been together for ten years in all, married for five.

I moved out my Steinway grand piano, while Linda moved in with singer P.P. Arnold. The house was eventually sold, although it was slightly perplexing as, initially, the realtor wouldn't tell me who was buying the property and would only refer to the mystery buyer as 'B.S.' Yes, I did wonder if it this was indeed all B.S., but it turned out to be Bruce Springsteen.

Years later, I was walking my red setter, Brian, in the streets above Sunset Boulevard when a dirt bike went past and then made a quick U-turn. I was a bit nervous as I was alone apart from Brian who was a world-famous coward. The bike zoomed over to me and skidded to a stop. The rider was wearing a full-face helmet and so his identity was completely concealed. Who is that masked man? I thought.

He then pushed up his visor.

'Hiya Jim, I thought it was you,' said Bruce. 'Nice dog.'

'You nearly gave me a heart attack. I thought you were going to grab my wallet,' I replied.

'No, I'm OK for cash,' the Boss smiled.

'How are you settling in?' I asked.

'It's great. I turned the guest apartment into a studio and am working on some songs.'

And with a few other pleasantries he lowered the visor and, with a wave, was on his way.

I had met Bruce at a St Patrick's Day party with Rod. He and Bruce had eyed each other and nodded but didn't communicate. Bruce was quiet, shy and slightly introverted. His stage persona was completely different from his offstage character. At the end of the evening as were waiting for the valet to bring us our cars, we got into a conversation about automobiles. We hung out later at Rod's beach house and Bruce remarked, 'I've been in the studio and just listened back to what I've done. I have great arrangements, but no songs.' And he scrapped them. One song I'm glad – as is the world – that he didn't scrap was 'Born in the USA', which he told me he'd written in my old house. I like to think it was inspired by my clear plastic toilet seat with a circle of barbed wire embedded in it.

One of my closest mates is fellow guitarist Robin Le Mesurier. You'll probably have heard of him through his own illustrious career, but you'll also have heard of his thespian parents, John Le Mesurier and Hattie Jacques. Robin experienced a very bohemian background, growing up in Earl's Court in the 1960s where the family home was a haven for Spike Milligan, Peter Sellers, Kenneth Williams and others too humorous to mention.

Robin and I first met when I was recording with Cockney Rebel. Steve Harley had also asked him to join the band, but Robin had a thing about clowns and refused to wear a clown's outfit. In fact, it was only Steve who donned a red nose – there was no other paraphernalia involved. (But it always makes me laugh that Robin was happy to dress up as a Womble!) Robin is a guitarist I have always admired – he has feel, soul, skill and style and so I was delighted when he joined Rod's band in 1981.

Robin was great fun with a very dry sense of humour and quickly became an integral part of the band, not only onstage but he also took part in all our shenanigans and antics – of which there were plenty. As long as we were all professional in our work, nothing else was taken too seriously. We used to rehearse in Rod's garage at his house on Carolwood Drive. It was a pretty swanky neighbourhood and inevitably some of the neighbours were a bit put out by the racket. Luckily the next door houseowner was much more welcoming. He was happy to listen to the band and used to come and watch us rehearse. In fact, he was such a generous neighbour that he and his wife cut a hole in the fence so that Rod and I could use their tennis court whenever we liked. Yes, Gregory Peck was definitely one of the good guys. After one LA show, I joined him and Fred Astaire in the green room for a drink and somewhat incredibly, the great dancer asked me, 'Who does your choreography?' I replied in astonishment, 'We make it up as we go along. But it's mainly spontaneous falling over.'

Mr Astaire might have been referring to a routine that Rod started one night.

'You know that bit where I jump on to the piano? As I come off and run across the stage, you crouch down and I'll jump over you.'

'OK, I know,' I said, entering into the spirit of the thing. 'I can pretend I've dropped my plectrum,' wondering if my lurid green, vinyl trousers could withstand the strain. Initially, this worked successfully, but on the third night, Rod skidded to a halt beside me and said, 'Come on Jim, stop mucking about. People have paid good money to see this show.' He reprised this trick the last time we played together in 2015 in Hyde Park, but this time in front of a live audience of 55,000 and millions of television viewers. In the final verse of 'I was Only Joking', he sank to his knees and, grabbing me by the back of my jacket, pulled me down beside him. This was OK until he sang the final line when he leapt to his feet, leaving me on the floor to play the last bar of music. He then reached down and pretended to help me up as if I was incapable of getting up unaided. I got my revenge by giving him a hefty shove across the stage, which I hope let everyone know that there was life in the old dog yet.

After I split with Linda in 1981, I was on the *Tonight I'm Yours* tour, aptly subtitled, 'Worth leaving Home For' and in mid-November, we were playing in Florida. We were often invited to after-show parties and, on this occasion, we were invited to a reception at Turnberry Isle, a luxury tennis and golf resort in Aventura. I did notice, being a professional nautical nuisance, that there seemed to be some large, elegant boats in the harbour and there was one luxurious and even more enormous yacht that caught my eye.

I was introduced to a young Arab guy named Omar who offered to take me on board this super yacht and introduce me to some of his friends. There was one, in particular, who took my attention immediately — it must have been something to do with her enormous, liquid brown eyes, sexy Italian accent and innate beauty. Sheika Dena Al-Fassi was a stunning woman who had married into the Saudi royal family. I was immediately smitten. Something clicked right away, and we talked and laughed until dawn. She spoke English and French along with Arabic. This was the beginning of an affair that lasted more than a year and was the most complicated romance of my life.

Diana, as she was known, told me that she was getting a divorce from her husband Sheik Mohammed. His sister had married a Saudi prince and so he, Diana and their relatives became members of the Saudi royal family. For the divorce settlement she had hired Marvin 'Marriage with no rings attached' Mitchelson as her divorce attorney. He was a flamboyant showbiz lawyer, known as the 'Prince of Palimony' and Mitchelson had suggested that Diana should sue for $3 billion, half of Mohammed's alleged wealth. The court case had elicited a great deal of publicity.

I had no idea when we met that there was anything like this going on and, as is often the case, money in huge quantities messes things up. Mohammed and Diana had four children, two of their own and two adopted. She told me that he didn't want any more to do with her, but just the same, had arranged for two ex-SAS, heavily armed bodyguards to accompany her everywhere. An aide warned me from pursuing Diana, and that I might also be at risk, but this made me more interested in her, although I slept with a sharp wit and pointed remark close by – just in case.

We began to meet secretly at her house on Sunset Boulevard and Diana would also come to see us play in various cities around United States. She used to follow the tour around in a private jet, accompanied by an entourage consisting of her personal secretary, hairdresser and beautician … and the two bodyguards. Of course, the band members were intrigued and found great humour in the situation. When we were talking about the fast-approaching Christmas holidays and they were asked what they wanted as gifts, 'Matching helicopters' was the pre-planned and coordinated answer from them all. Diana also used a bigger stretch limousine than Rod's, which he found highly amusing.

Anyway, Diana and I decided to go skiing in the mountains outside Pittsburgh. I think one of her party knew the area, so we rented a house above the snow line for a week. It was beautiful, very remote and quiet. One day, I was chatting with Martin and Gary, the two bodyguards, when they asked me if I had ever shot a pistol.

'No,' I replied.

'Well, we can show you, let's take a walk up here into the woods and teach you.'

So, this is it. Martin and Gary had been paid off. And I was in for 'The Long Goodbye'. There'll be a nasty accident, I'll be thrown down a crevasse and won't be found till spring. What have I done?

'Oh God, please, No … not here … not like this,' a voice in my head screamed.

'Come on then,' Gary says.

'We'll bring this big cardboard box as a target,' Martin gave a knowing look to Gary.'

Box! What are they going to do with that box?

So, the condemned man put one foot in front of the other and staggered up the hill.

'Hey, what's it like playing with Rod Stewart?' asks Gary.

Ahah. Trying to me lull into a false sense of security.

'Yeah it's great!' I give the standard reply. They want me to die with happy thoughts.

Martin is scouring the landscape, 'This'll do, Jim take the box and lean it up against that bank over there.'

Should I make a run for it?

I'm rooted with fear and trapped by my indecision.

'Ok give it to me, I'll do it,' says Martin and pulls the box away from me and places it on the bank.

'Here we go,' says Gary and whips out his out his Glock.

Next thing I know he's leaning over me saying, 'Jim! You ok?'

'Must be the altitude,' I say as they help me to my feet. 'I came over all dizzy.'

'So, let's shoot at that box and pretend it's that asshole of a husband,' grins Martin.

And we did. The box never recovered. In fact, Mohammed al-Fassi, 'that asshole of a husband', died in Cairo in 2002 – not from gunshot wounds, but from an infected hernia.

The band were playing in San Francisco and Diana took the presidential suite at the Fairmont, an extremely luxurious hotel atop Nob Hill where we were staying. There was access from a private elevator in the lobby. The suite had a swimming pool, a two-storey galleried library, an observatory and a dining room which could seat twenty-eight people. And just in case of a domestic emergency, there was also a twenty-four-hour butler and maid service. The enormous living room had a grand piano and I suggested we throw a party. Most of the band and crew were there and the highlight of the evening was John Le Mesurier, Robin's actor dad, entertaining us until the early hours with Noel Coward standards like 'London Pride' and 'A Room with a View'.

The affair with Diana ended very sadly. Mohammed took the children away from her, which sent her into a spiral of despair. Diana's sister-in-law was into some heavy drugs and Diana, herself, became influenced in that direction. Diana's brother managed to access some of her money and bought himself a castle on the proceeds. He also persuaded Diana that I was no good for her and that there would be no future with a rock musician. They were all living in the disused guest house hidden at the back of the Sunset Boulevard mansion. I was never invited and just could glimpse it from a side gate. There were no mobile phones in those days, so private calls were impossible. Diana's lifestyle, her family's antipathy and all the publicity about her divorce had naturally affected our relationship.

These outside influences were tearing her apart and she didn't seem to trust anyone any more. I decided to call it off. I wrote to her saying that it was too painful for me to continue our affair. Not an easy letter to write but without more time together I could feel it slipping away. For months afterwards I looked for her in all the old haunts, but she seemed to have completely disappeared.

Years later, when I had remarried, the phone rang. A familiar voice inquired, without any greeting, 'What do you mean by this letter?'

I knew immediately it was her. Slightly stunned for words, I paused before replying, 'You're a bit late with your response.'

'Well what do you mean by it?' she repeated. She sounded genuinely upset that I had called it off. To deflect the question, I asked where she was.

'In Egypt, seeing my children. This is the only country where we can meet. If I go to Saudi, they'll keep me there.'

What a disaster this part of her life had become. If only she had told me that she needed more time. Much later, after becoming sober, she settled quietly back in Italy and I'm happy to say she re-married and is doing well. We are friends on Facebook. It's safer that way.

Meanwhile my rock and roll lifestyle continued. We were flying around the world in private jets (we used two private Lear jets to travel and nicknamed one of them 'The Flying Ashtray' – for the smokers amongst us), riding in luxury limos, and there was inevitably much foolish behaviour. Life on the road was never dull – due in part to the formation of 'Sex Police', a sort of gang of alter egos, formed by band members, roadies, crew and various reprobates. Rod described it pretty well:

> Our founding intention was to stamp out sex on the road – to identify, within the touring party, the likely practitioners of sex, locate the places in which sex might take place and prevent sex from happening ... even the Sex Police feared a knock on the door from the Sex Police.

Crudelis Sed Justi: this was the slogan we had emblazoned across specially made T-shirts for the band, which translated as 'Cruel But Fair'. Cruel, yes. Fair, I'm not sure about. The commando-like operations involved gaffer taping fellow band members to beds, emptying their hotel rooms of furniture and other nefarious activities. We all had nicknames – Robin was known as Gruppenführer (group leader) and because of my love of sailing I was given the name of 'Seaman Stains'. Other members were 'Corporal Punishment', 'Major Bucks' (Rod) and 'Private Parts'.

In his 2017 autobiography, *A Charmed Rock 'N' Roll Life*, Robin Le Mesurier wrote:

> The Sex Police was an organisation to be feared by all ... band members were chained to beds, the contents of hotel rooms were emptied into lifts and bedroom doors were removed. As time went by our 'missions' became more varied and imaginative. We wore

white boiler suits when we went to work, carried toolkits and screwdrivers for more complex operations, hid walkie-talkies about our bodies, secreted cameras for evidence purposes and indulged in the use of ropes and handcuffs whenever necessary.

Any of us might approach the hotel reception and demand several of the room keys, belonging to the band, to which the receptionist would usually reply, 'No, I'm sorry, we can't do that, sir.'

'But I need at least three other keys!'

'I can only give you your own key.'

'But I need them.'

'Why do you need them, sir?'

'For the Sex Police.'

'I don't understand, we don't have sex police here.'

'Oh yes, you do ...'

Nakedness and rudeness were an integral part of the band's high jinks.

One of our crew, 'Boiler', was particularly prone to stripping off for no apparent reason, stating 'I'll do anything to stay in showbiz.'

Part of our entourage was Louise Fisher, who started doing hair and make-up for Rod, but eventually became the group's matriarch. Louise was great – well spoken and educated, she was an English rose. On the surface you would imagine this would not necessarily be a good match with the rowdiness of us lot and her apparent quiet reserve. Wrong. She was completely un-shockable and took everything in her stride. She became a secret member of the Sex Police and had the greatest sense of humour. This was stretched to the limit when we rather unkindly noticed she occasionally received mail from her fiancé, actor Richard Hope. The Sex Police steamed open one such love letter and added all our names below Richard's signature. 'Cruel but Fair'. We watched with interest as she opened it and realised that we had all perused the missive.

'Love from Jim, Rod, Robin, Kevin etc.,' she read. Blushing furiously, she admonished us. 'You boys! I'll have to tell Dicky not to write any more if you're all going to read the letters.'

'Oh no!' we chorused. 'Don't do that. We'll leave your mail alone.' And we did, because we loved her. But she told us later that Dicky started his letters, 'Dearest Louise, and Jim, Rod, Robin, et al' ... just in case.

We went through a phase of removing our trousers when we went out to dinner – if there was a tablecloth long enough to cover our pale skinny legs. 'Why oh why?' you may ask and all I can offer is ... it seemed like a good idea at the time. In a similar vein, I remember sitting at a counter at Benihana's steak and knife-juggling restaurant in 'Heavily Bills' with about six of my bandmates when somebody suggested we all link arms and then deliberately fall backwards off our barstools. This was part of an ongoing game called 'Nasty Accident', which I think we inherited from the Faces. The ensuing chaos as people leaped out of the way while we thrashed about on the floor trying not to laugh too much and checking for broken bones deemed it a fair description. It generally only required lots of people in the heap on the floor all shouting, 'Nasty accident! There's been a nasty accident!' for it to be a successful ruse and to be oft repeated. Of course, we generally got thrown out at that stage. On Kevin Savigar's stag night we surpassed ourselves by getting chucked out of at least ten establishments and the pandemonium was nicely achieved another time when a TV film crew waited at the airport as the tour jet taxied up and the entire band hurled themselves down the exit stairs and lay writhing on the tarmac shouting, 'There's been a nasty accident!'

My elbow still hurts.

We played in Japan on a few tours and there was one particular club in Tokyo called the Lexington Queen, which we frequented whenever possible. It seemed that most of the female models visiting Tokyo would spend time there, which we found of interest. On our nights off – which were few – we could be found there, talent spotting. Everywhere we went in Japan, Rod was accompanied by a heavily muscled bodyguard who we called 'Tojo'. I don't like racial stereotypes, but I have to say he was archetypically inscrutable. Rod and I found ourselves in the company of two lovely American girls who shared an apartment nearby. Breaking all touring rules which stipulate you must always return to the hotel with guests or strangers, we walked up the rickety staircase to a small flat with one double and one single bedroom. My 'friend' Theresa had the double room. Rod took one look at his accommodation and decided it wasn't conducive for romance and decided to head for the hotel with his 'friend'.

I realised that the flat overlooked the street below so, grabbing a large bowl I filled it with water and opened the window. Below Tojo was just opening the car door for Rod and the mystery model. I hurled the water out the window, but I was a bit out of practice and this, coupled with Rod's inherent good fortune, meant that I missed him and hit Tojo, who immediately went into full martial arts pose, his hands in defensive karate position, his eyes swivelling, and ready to leap into action. The only sound was Rod's voice from inside the car, 'You bastard Cregan, I'll get you for this.' Even though I was crouching down and hidden from view, I ventured, 'It wasn't me, honest.' Rod's reply, 'Oh yeah, tell Tojo that,' wasn't reassuring.

Tojo never did get the chance to exact revenge. That was left to Rod and the other band members, who from then on continually laced my sake with vodka. They would pretend to drink as much as me but they either filled their glasses with water or surreptitiously emptied the contents when I wasn't watching. I couldn't understand why I was getting so drunk while everyone else remained sober. I haven't drunk sake since. Another avenue of pleasure cut off.

On days off, we would try to find a top-notch restaurant and occasionally would be designated a private room. For no apparent reason we invented 'The Downstairs Supper Club', which worked best when the dining table had long tablecloths reaching down to the floor. We would scramble under the table, accompanied by our drinks, ice buckets and bottles of wine, a couple of candles, and would lie comfortably on the floor, and carry on conversing. We could hear the waiters bringing the next course wondering what had happened to us and where we had gone. As soon as they had left, we would emerge and send someone out to make a complaint about the service and demand to know what had happened to our next course. When asked where we had been, we would reply, 'Just dropped in to the downstairs supper club.'

Carmine Appice was fired from the band when Rod discovered he had made a deal with the two new guys he had introduced to the band. He had agreed with them that he would get a percentage for anything that they wrote for Rod! No one had ever heard of such a ridiculous idea. He claims that he was replaced because he wanted a production credit, but he was never even in the running. On two of the big hits, 'Tonight I'm Yours' and 'Young Turks', he was rarely in the studio. In fact, we used a drum machine with maybe Carmine playing a hi-hat live. Almost everything was played by Kevin, Robin and me. I have seen Carmine a few times since those days and he's mellowed rather well. We seem to be OK. When producer Tom Dowd left, Rod asked me to help him finish producing the record. I was the only one, apart from the engineer, who was in the studio when Rod was singing. He kindly declared that I was good at helping him get that extra something out of his vocal performance.

On most occasions on tour we would all be sharing the same hotel floor and in the same order along the corridor, so we were usually next to the same band member. However, this time at the Carlton Hotel in Cannes, France, I found myself next door to the brilliant Tony Brock, who had replaced Carmine. We noticed our rooms had an adjoining door which we immediately opened in the spirit of community, friendship and ... partying. The Carlton is a beautiful old hotel which has played host to many film stars and dignitaries and is considered the jewel of the French Riviera. The League of

Nations, the precursor to the United Nations, was negotiated here in 1922. Lloyd George stayed in the presidential suite, now renamed after some film star.

Our third-floor rooms were slightly more humble and looked out over a side street. I think we might have tried to go to our beds for some shuteye but at around 3 a.m. I found myself wide awake and heard Tony making a racket in his room. Dressed only in the luxurious white towelling bath robes provided by the hotel, we decided to party on. As a disclaimer I would like to offer the very feeble excuse that Tony and I might have had a tiny bit too much to drink and the two of us were having such fun that we accidentally guzzled the entire contents of my minibar. We were dancing and singing and generally being rowdy when I realised the minibar was empty.

'Bloody hell,' I remarked. 'This fridge is useless. It's empty. Let's get rid of it. Let's put it out on the balcony.'

'Good idea. It's taking up far too much room sitting there against the wall and it's beginning to annoy me,' said Tony. We manhandled the fridge through the *fin de siècle* French doors and on to the Romeo and Juliet balcony. 'Merde,' I said coming over all native. 'It's too big. I won't be able to close the doors. What a kind of balcony is it that won't take a fridge? I know, let's push it over the railing and into the street. No one will notice it's gone.'

With a surprising show of strength, I grabbed the fridge and although admittedly staggering a bit, I managed to perch it on the railing. Suddenly, without any warning, Tony came over all sensible.

'Hang on a sec. It's not just going to land in the flowerbed. There is a very good chance it will hit that Maserati.'

'No, it won't, I'm sure it will miss it,' I replied. But then hazily remembering that I had been arrested in Florida for a vaguely similar adventure, I reconsidered. Rats!

'Oh well, maybe that's not so clever. I suppose we better put it back.'

After returning the fridge to its rightful place I spotted a small breakfast tray with the remains of my breakfast. It had been two boiled eggs, but they had been too runny for my delicate palate and I couldn't eat them. Somehow, they flew through the air and connected with the wall about 10ft up.

'Best place for them,' I muttered.

'What we need is some music,' suggested Tony.

Everybody in those days carried a boombox so, to the strains of 'Brown Sugar', we started to dance. It became a kind of conga, through my room, out the door, along the corridor, into Tony's room and back around. Then there had been some foolish dancing in the style of Eric Morecambe whilst wearing a flasher's mac. With both hands in the pockets you brought one side of the mac across your body, then rapidly switched sides covering your rude bits in the process. We did this in time to the music as we stumbled about in our bath robes. Eventually this attracted the attention of another guest who stuck his head out the door and gave us what for in French.

By this time, we were starting to flag and retired to our rooms where we crashed out. The first thing I noticed when I woke were the two eggs firmly adhered to the wall. That looks a bit nasty, I thought. Maybe I should get a knife and try to scrape them off. I found a suitable chair and, forgetting that I was still naked, climbed up and started to remove yesterday's breakfast in the hope that I would not be charged for redecorating the room. Talk about treading on egg shells. Whilst at full stretch I heard the communicating door open and Tony entered, remarking, 'I know you're hungry, but they are probably a bit cold by now. I was thinking of going down to get some breakfast myself. Although the sight of your naked bum has put me off a bit.'

On departure Tony was handed his extras bill.

'What's this extra 250 francs for?' he asked the desk clerk.

'That's for your extra room sir.'

'Only had one room,' said Tony, indignantly.

'Yes, but the gentleman who was kept awake all night refused to pay for his room,' The receptionist raised a haughty eyebrow. 'He also commented that you were dancing naked in the corridor.'

'Ahh yes,' replied Tony sheepishly. 'I had forgotten about that.'

So, we split the cost of the extra room between us. Cheap at the price when you think the alternative might have been acquiring a gleaming new Maserati. It's funny how hotels bring out the worst in people.

We spent a couple of months recording *Tonight I'm Yours* at the Record Plant, the legendary LA studio. Next door was a restaurant called L'Entourage, where we had a direct telephone line from the studio where we could be contacted if needed to lay down an over-dub or a solo. Kevin Savigar described the scene as, 'Like spitfire pilots scrambling for their planes when the call went out that they were needed at the studio.'

Chris Stone owned the Record Plant and was the most generous and accommodating man. Musicians loved to hang out there as he was very tolerant of some of the antics of some of the artists who had recorded there over the years. If there was any damage to the equipment or the studio itself (I'm mainly talking Keith Moon here) Chris wouldn't give them a hard time; he would simply add the cost of the repairs to the studio fees.

Chris, who sadly passed away in 2016, would stop at nothing in making us feel welcome and comfortable. When he realised that we were spending so much time at L'Entourage, he built us our own 'pub' at the studio, which we named the Dog and Clit. To make it as authentic as possible, we installed a dart board by the front door. Various other artists would drop by for a drink and a game of darts.

One of these visitors was Bobby Womack, the elegant and charming soul singer. We were engaged in a friendly game of darts and playing 'closest to the bull' when I noticed my old 'throwing knife' tucked away in the corner of the bar. This had been given to me by the lads as a birthday present sometime before. It was monstrous, about a foot in length, and I used to practice with it backstage during those boring times before sound check. Bobby had just placed a dart quite close to the bullseye. Turning to me with a smile he said, 'Your turn.' Surreptitiously, I picked up the knife and threw it at the board. You know some days, you just can't do anything wrong? Well, this was one of those days. The knife hurtled into the bullseye, impaling the board to the wall. I returned Bobby's smile with interest, 'I think I'm closest.' If it was humanly possible, he would have turned white.

We used to arrive about midday and sit around coming up with ideas and making suggestions about the songs we were recording. We treated the recordings seriously, but, as ever, there was time for some shenanigans. On one occasion, Robin unscrewed the top of Rod's microphone and inserted a piece of sushi. Rod, quite quickly, began to notice something fishy was going on but couldn't work out where quite quickly the malodorous smell was coming from. He ended up sniffing his clothing and everything around him trying to figure it out. Of course, everyone else knew what had gone on. This continued for a day or two until we relented, having congratulated each other on what we considered a particularly good scheme.

One night, after finishing at about 1 a.m., Rod suggested that I come back to his house for a nightcap.

'Alana's having one of her parties and you might find it amusing,' says he with a knowing look. We were a bit scruffy for an 'A list' party, but we couldn't care less, and I sensed a certain pleasure in him inviting me. Alana thought of the band as 'staff' and wouldn't be best pleased. When Rod and I entered the party room I quickly realised that Alana and I really did have something in common … we were the only ones that were not household names. In fact, I was the only person I didn't recognise.

Cher was off to one side dancing alone and happily ignoring everyone, actor Ryan O'Neal wanted to talk music and was very informed, knowing lots more than me, while David Janssen, of *The Fugitive* fame, was chilling at the bar, as only he could.

But it was Liza Minnelli who really wanted to rock. Somehow, I found myself playing flamenco guitar while she danced with a rose clamped between her teeth ... or were those my teeth? Wilder and faster, she turned and swayed, stamping her feet in time to my outlandish attempt to play while suffering the effects of Martini poisoning. So, I abandon the guitar and swept her round the room, attempting unsuccessfully to avoid the tiger skin rug, complete with massive head that invariably caught unsuspecting guests by the ankle and deposited them on the floor in a heap. Liza took all this very well. She had a great sense of humour and all her inhibitions had long since been removed. I guess that's what happens when you're the daughter of Judy Garland and raised in Hollywood.

Meanwhile, a grinning Tony Curtis was dancing with a dining chair, spinning it around his body. He offered me a lesson. I couldn't say no and didn't want to. It looks easy, but as you spin the chair on one leg and try to jive with it, it deliberately attacks you with its other legs causing the kind of bruises that on examination the following morning, you remark, 'Where the hell did these come from?'

Alana had gone AWOL at some stage during the frolics but reappeared holding the infant Kimberley in her arms.

'Look what you've done, you've woken the baby!'

Hmmm ... the nursery was at the other end of this huge mansion and on another floor. There was no way that we could have woken the baby. We all stared at our feet and looked sheepishly at each other, trying not to laugh.

We were all unceremoniously sent home in disgrace. But it was definitely worth it.

There was group of ex-pat British actors who were employed in the Los Angeles movie studios in the 1920s and 1930s. Mainly upper class, their presence harked back to the days of colonialism and the Empire, and who collectively became known as the 'Hollywood Raj'. The troupe extended the notion beyond just socialising. When Laurence Olivier checked into the Chateau Marmont Hotel, there was a note awaiting his arrival which read, 'There will be net practice tomorrow at 4 p.m. I trust I shall see you there.' It came from Sir C. Aubrey Smith, founder of the Hollywood cricket eleven, whose other members included Errol Flynn, David Niven and Boris Karloff.

The members of the band, partners, associates and various guests continued this tradition half a century later. Except we didn't play cricket. That would have been taking the whole thing too far. But we did meet every Sunday night for dinner. Robin Le Mesurier says that he started this ritual, but I think it was me. We weren't trying to further ourselves in the Hollywood firmament – it was nothing to do with business as this weekly event was simply arranged to have fun and keep some sort of British thing going. Everyone would take it in turns to cook (until we got lazy and started to hire chefs). We would always convene at 8 p.m. and usually produced the same meal – a roast leg of lamb with all the trimmings, although I occasionally would poach a salmon, to a chorus of disapproval from the traditionalists.

Apart from the usual suspects, we used to invite various waifs and strays. Robert Palmer was a regular, as was Michael Crawford, who was very funny and a great piss taker. Billy Connolly, who I met through B.A. Robertson, joined us on occasions. I love him. Hilarious, but also a great listener. Billy wasn't at all competitive and loved to laugh at our jokes, which of course endeared him to the gang even more. His observational routines are beautifully constructed, so clever and my favourite type of comedy, typified by this one-liner: 'I've always wanted to go to Switzerland to see what the army does with those wee red knives.'

6

Bun Fight at the OK Kraal

Before I got into rock n' roll, I was going to be a dentist.

Gregg Allman

In 1983 Rod had broken up with Alana and was renting a house in a gated community in Beverly Hills. He wasn't in the best of spirits and so I suggested he come and stay with me. I had a spare room, a jacuzzi and plenty of wine. Rod stayed for four months and we rubbed along together nicely. He was, however, an early riser and would become bored, waiting for me to get up, so very occasionally, he would bring me a cup of tea in bed in the morning and would point out, 'I bet Elvis never did this.' To which I would reply, 'You're right, the last time Elvis was here, he couldn't get off the toilet.'

Rod used to collect his kids from school and take them back to the Carolwood house. Apart from his dutiful devotion to his children, Rod's time was also spent with his latest love, Texan model Kelly Emberg. Rod and I were thinking of buying an apartment in New

York and so we shuffled off to the Big Apple and stayed in Kelly's place in Greenwich Village.

Through Kelly Emberg, I met Joanne Russell, another model. She was absolutely stunning and, true to form, I fell for her. I reckon we dated, although Jo probably wouldn't call it dating. I'd also like to think she fell for me – but she didn't. All right, we were 'just good friends'. Anyway, while I was in New York, Stevie Wonder was performing in a concert at Radio City Music Hall. The four of us had a box near the back of the hall. Stevie hears that Rod is in the hall and announces this to the audience. He introduces Rod.

'Stand up Rod, give us a wave.'

Rod is still married and doesn't want to be seen with Kelly at this stage and so lays low. Stevie encourages one of the crew to find Rod, using a searchlight. Rod slumps in his seat, desperately trying to stay out the spotlight – literally. Stevie gives up, but later he starts playing and singing, 'Do You think I'm Sexy?' Rod is now lying on the floor. Stevie wouldn't give it up. 'Come on Rod, don't be shy.'

Stevie kept calling for him, but Rod wouldn't show himself. There was only one thing to do. We scarpered.

Another trip to New York started out with a quiet lunch in Hollywood with our saxophone and harmonica player Jimmy Zavala and his beautiful wife, Shelley. Halfway through some pasta and a rather nice bottle of red I remembered that a very old friend of mine, Jimmy Horowitz, had written a musical, called *Marlowe*, which was to be produced in New York. I'd thought at first it was about Raymond Chandler's hard-bitten detective, Philip Marlowe, but it turned out to be based on the life of Elizabethan playwright Christopher Marlowe. Of course, the dramatist might have been equally hard bitten, as there was a lot to be cynical about in the sixteenth century, but this is neither here nor there. Anyway, the show was opening the next day on Broadway. This was a big deal. It's incredibly hard to get anything made that will open on Broadway. You normally have to start in an insignificant town in the theatre above a public toilet.

'What kind of friend am I?' I thought.

'Useless,' came the swift reply.

'Hey guys, my old pal has an opening in New York tomorrow and I really want to be there. Do you fancy a weekend in NYC?'

'Yeah, that sounds like fun.'

'Let's finish our lunch and get over there!'

I cannot remember, for the life of me, why I didn't go home and grab a few things. Instead we drove straight to the airport and I bought three first-class tickets. On the way I used my new primitive car phone to book a hotel and arranged for a car to meet us.

'We'll just buy some toiletries when we get there.'

At this point in my career I was the living embodiment of the adage, 'A fool and his money are welcome everywhere.' Clutching our new toothbrushes, we check into the hotel. It's late and we're tired. All that free champagne on the plane has taken its toll.

The next morning, we head off to a tuxedo rental shop nearby. We hire everything, including a couple of extra shirts. Shelley opts for a black tailcoat while Jimmy and I are in regular dinner jackets. Reconvening back in the hotel lobby, dressed in our penguin suits, we are milling about by the entrance to the formal dining room. Standing slightly to one side of the others I am approached by an elderly gentleman.

'Good afternoon, I'm George Blenkinsop. We have a reservation for two at 1 p.m.' He is accompanied by his mistress, secretary, daughter, cousin, godchild or therapist, but certainly not his wife.

'Ah yes, Mr Blenkinsop. We are expecting you, please come this way.'

Grabbing a couple of menus, I sweep them into the dining room, through the chattering crowds to an empty table.

'Your waiter will be with you shortly. I hope you enjoy your lunch.' I bow, obsequiously, giving my best Basil Fawlty impression. To my amusement I find a $20 bill being pressed into my hand. 'This seems like a very good racket,' I think to myself, as I attempt to grab another waiting couple. But before I can give it a second try, I feel a hand upon my shoulder. The real maître d' has spotted me.

'Very funny, sir,' he snarls through gritted teeth. 'Are you a guest in the hotel?'

'Yes, I am, actually, and you seemed rather busy, so I thought I would help out. I'm just here for my wedding,' I added, hoping to circumvent calls for hotel security, 'so no hard feelings, I hope?' and I extend my hand, unfortunately forgetting it still contained the $20 bill. As if magnetised, the money leapt onto his palm and a chilling grin appeared. But just on his teeth, it never reached his eyes, as cold as pebbles on a winter beach.

Forgoing eating in the hotel, we ventured out into Manhattan and discovered that people treat you completely differently if you are dressed in a tuxedo. We had hired wing collar shirts and those strange little starched white cotton pique waistcoats that have no back, so in general we were not mistaken for waiters, but rather people celebrating something fantastic.

So, we lied our way through the afternoon, varying our roles from actors taking a break from filming to funeral pallbearers or gate crashers at a society wedding. We might have visited a bar or two and as the pretend bridegroom, with best man and woman in tow, we were generally treated to free refreshments ...

We enjoyed *Marlowe* and repaired to the after party which was bustling and noisy. The music business was well represented and for some reason I found myself sitting across a table from David Lee Roth, the flamboyant lead singer for Van Halen. With my relatively short hair and tuxedo it was easy for me to continue my role as anything but a rock musician.

'Aren't you David Lee Roth?' I asked in my best British accent.

'Yes, I am,' agreed David with a smile.

'Wow, this is great! I've never met a rock singer before. What's it like being up there on that stage in front of all those people? It must be amazing.' And David, bless him, answered every question with his famous sense of humour.

So essentially, I interviewed him for about twenty minutes, about life in a rock band, the touring, recording in studios, groupies and anything else I could think of. Eventually, I rose to my feet and extending my hand, I pulled him gently towards me. Whispering in his ear I said, 'Thanks Dave. By the way, I'm Jim Cregan, and I'm lead guitarist with Rod Stewart and have been playing with him for about ten years. Nice to meet you at last.'

The look on his face was enough to make coming to New York worthwhile. And as I melted back into the crowd, he shook his fist at me.

'Bastard!' he mouthed.

In August 1983, the band was in Sun City, the South African casino resort. There was some suggestion that we were supporting apartheid just by being there but there was no apartheid at Sol's place. The audiences were mixed, there was no segregation and local black men and women were in positions of authority and responsibility. Sun City provided meaningful, well-paid jobs for South Africans of all colours, but anyone who played there was given a hard time. On our nights off we foolishly spent our time losing our money in the 'salle privée', which was beautifully managed by an elegant black guy named Ben.

The complex was the brainchild of Sol Kerzner, who claimed to have had it built from scratch in the middle of a semi-desert. And whatever the political undertones, Sol Kerzner turned it into an oasis. He was married to the stunningly beautiful Anneline Kriel, a former Miss World, who came out with us to dinner on more than one occasion and, I seem to remember, to prove quite how seductive she could be, surreptitiously removed her underwear and tossed it into the breadbasket.

Playing Sun City was pretty good fun except on Saturdays we had to play two shows in the evening – one at around five and the next one about nine. This was pretty weird and none of us had ever done this before. It was a ninety-minute show and generally by the time you're finished you are at a tired but euphoric stage when refreshments are much required. But not there or then. I discovered the best way to deal with the schedule was to finish the show, have a shower, get into bed, have a nap, set the alarm and on waking, take another shower and pretend it was a completely different day. A sort of 'Groundhog Day' in reverse. I reckon that the only way to combat weirdness is to be even weirder.

On the plus side we had loads of time off. We had shows on Thursday through Sunday, leaving three days for fun. On one of these breaks, Sol generously offered us his house in Cape Town. For some reason he had taken a shine to us. The house was a short walk from the beach and had riding stables and land to explore. There was a huge rusting wreck of a freighter caught on the rocks and it brought home to us the dangers of the Cape, here where the Atlantic meets the Indian ocean and all hell breaks loose on a stormy night.

Anyway, Elton John was wondering if he should also play Sun City, so he came for a visit while we were there and decided to join us on safari. 'Us' was Rod and a young blonde, his assistant, Don Archell, yours truly and a young redhead, Kevin Savigar and his lovely wife Sue. Elton arrived in full splendour, accompanied by his personal assistant Bob Halley, at MalaMala – a game reserve that can only be reached by small plane. Well, it had to be small because there's no runway as such – just a clearing in the jungle, or at least that's what it seemed like to me. A couple of open-topped Land Rovers sped alongside us as we screeched safely to a halt, in a cloud of dust. There was fortunately no 'nasty accident'.

The athletic, muscle-bound MalaMala crew were dressed in full Hollywood safari gear with wide hats, beige shorts, socks and shirts, sturdy brown boots and revolvers on their belts. Above the Land Rover dashboards, their rifles were fixed in readiness. Elton immediately started swooning at the sight of these hunky guys and was inevitably soon in love with at least three of them.

We took the short drive to the main compound where we found a little shop, which sold very similar outfits to the rangers. There was a lot of pushing and shoving as we contested to buy the kit which would clearly turn us into seasoned explorers. Those who had never experienced the Harrods' sale, and were a little slow off the mark, ended up with ill-fitting, oversized shorts and socks and battered, ancient hats, which looked like they had been relinquished by Lord Baden-Powell and some scruffy boy scouts. This was to be a photographic safari – so true to the spirit of adventure I had purchased a telephoto lens the size of an elephant's penis. A fat lot of good it did me as most of my shots turned out to be over exposed and generally useless. I am going to blame old South African film stock, but it was probably operator error.

MalaMala is a great mixture of the primitive and civilised. At first sight the circular, whitewashed mud huts with their grass roofs didn't look very welcoming but inside they were delightful, with air conditioning, useful double beds and hot showers. The contrast to the open-to-the-world exterior was dramatic, allowing any wild beast to wander between the huts. I'd never had a conversation with a buffalo before, but my imagination took over. I wanted to talk to the animals. I'd always fancied myself as a Dr Doolittle type.

'Morning, buffalo.'

'Morning, Cregan.'

'Hope you don't mind if I don't invite you in.'

'Fair enough. I do have a tendency to make a bit of a mess.'

'So, how is life in MalaMala?

'Mustn't grumble, Cregan. Although I expect you're here to see the lions, I suppose. No one comes to see us. And yet, did you know, we're one of "the big five"? We're quite sought after as trophies.'

'I'm not surprised', I replied before adding diplomatically, 'I like your horns.'

'Thanks, Cregan. Rather useful for goring actually.'

'Oh, I see.'

'No need to worry, Jim, if I may call you that. No, you see, according to the guide books we buffalos can be unpredictable and dangerous, but it's lazy journalism. We're really quite friendly. No, it's the crocodiles you want to be careful of.' The buffalo looked pensive. 'They can even take us out. I lost a second cousin last week. Sorely missed by friends and family. Anyway, I'd best be off. Bye, Jim.'

The buffalo wandered off towards Rod's hut, probably hoping for an autograph. I soon realised I was no Rex Harrison – I hadn't even asked the buffalo for his name. I walked slowly towards a river-bank and got chatting to one of Elton's love interests. Desperately attempting to appear nonchalant, I asked him, 'Umm ... so, is it really dangerous here?'

'No, we haven't had a fatality here for fifteen years.'

I tried to resist asking how long the place had been open, but curiosity got the better of me.

'What happened?'

'Ahh, a local chap was taken by a crocodile just along here. You really mustn't go within about 6ft of the bank to be on the safe side.'

Note to self: *never* go down to the river. Sixty feet might be more like it.

The ranger continued, wallowing in my nervousness. 'The crocs lie so still you can't see them and suddenly they leap out of the water and grab you so quickly you're gone in seconds. But they drown you, so you're not eaten alive.'

'Thank goodness for that,' I muttered. 'How considerate.' Suddenly feeling the need to go back to my hut and double lock the door, I said goodbye, vaguely wondering if the limp I was developing was from having my leg pulled so hard. I will never know.

The next day, as fresh as a used Kleenex, we set off to look for big game.

We were four to a Land Rover plus the ranger and 'a spotter' or tracker who sat in a strangely elevated chair perched on the back of the vehicle. There wasn't much to spot at first – other than large amounts of poop. Now, Elton and Rod described themselves as poop-ologists, taking great interest in the various deposits that we came across. But soon the tracker, sitting high up behind us, started to see lots of activity. He would make a low-pitched whistle to draw our attention to some animal in the bush. However, try as hard as I might and brandishing my telephoto lens, I only managed to see about a quarter of the things he mentioned.

We turned a corner on the track and, in a split second, we stumbled upon two lions stretched out in the sun. We weren't going very fast, so Mike, the ranger, stopped the Land Rover only 2 or 3ft away from them. Sue Savigar whispered desperately, 'Why are we stopping? Come on let's get out of here!' I was thinking the very same thing – only she got there first and so while inwardly panicking, I could pretend to be cool, whilst sitting about inches from a lion, which wasn't in a cage. Mike said quietly, 'There's no danger; they've just had their dinner and anyway for some reason they don't bother us when we're in the car.'

So we sat there for a while and after my terror had passed, I felt absolutely elated. Suddenly the two-way radio squawked incredibly loudly, 'Hey, Mike have you seen these leopards down by the pond?'

'Jesus!' I thought. 'Doesn't he know not to do that?' In my imagination the lions, having been disturbed from their slumber, might be looking around for some dessert. One beautiful, tawny eye opened for a second, stared right at me, slowly blinked and closed as he returned to his kip. Phew! Must have been some lunch.

Eventually we moved on and came to an open grassy space.

'I think there are some giraffes round here,' said Mike and, pulling off the track, he shouldered the rifle and stepped away from the vehicle. Whoosh! You would have thought we were a dance troop as we followed his choreography and mimicked his every step. Moving as one, we felt the need to be close to that rifle. Even though they tried very hard not to show it, I'm sure there's a certain amount of mischievous glee in scaring the pants off us townies, but I guess there isn't any other way to do it. Just take us for a stroll knowing that it's really quite safe.

The only time they showed any concern was in the presence of the elephants. They were feeding in amongst some trees. Mike told us to be quiet whilst he backed the Rover even nearer to them. They looked magnificent but, 'Were we a bit too close?' I asked. Mike reassured me and explained that the elephants give you a warning before they charge. Maybe a bit of semaphore or tapping some Morse code on a hollow log? No, they flap their ears and yell at you.

The next day, the lodge arranged for a barbecue way out in the bush near a crocodile-free shallow river. And boy, these guys know how to put on a spread. There were beautifully laid tables, with starched linen tablecloths, creaking with all kinds of delights. Fresh fish and game sizzled away on the barbecue – the aromatic smoke filling the air with delicious scents. A gazebo had been erected so we wouldn't turn too pink and the provision of comfortable directors' chairs provided the seating, allowing us to relax and unwind in this unspoiled country. They had thought of everything. Well everything … except for a loo. Discreetly I was handed a roll of toilet paper and told to find a bush. I didn't think much about it until, with my shorts around my ankles, a thought popped into my mind.

Snake.

What if there's a bloody snake?

I won't be able to run with my pants half off. So, I pulled one leg out of my pants in preparation for a semi-streak in case of a viper on the bum. Happily, there was no snake and I abluted as quickly as I ever had, although the memory still lingers to this day and so I don't like to linger on the toilet – just in case an adder has somehow found itself occupying my Dorset bathroom. MalaMala was one of those unforgettable experiences and the privilege of sharing it with some of my favourite people is about as good as it gets.

Oh yes, I forgot to mention, as we are a motley collection of flash buggers, we had decided to dress for dinner. I probably should explain that on these world tours you had to be prepared for any social occasion, so we had, in addition to our newly acquired safari kit, tennis gear, scuba stuff, summer and winter tuxedos, hiking boots, winter fur coats with silly Russian hats, skiing kit, and of course video players and cameras, plus assorted hi-fi and 'Sex Police' miscellaneous equipment, including walkie-talkies, handcuffs, toolkit and uniforms.

Much to our own amusement we went to dinner in black-tie. Elton of course was wearing a black tailcoat with an enormous brooch about the diameter of a hot cross bun which looked to the rest of us as if it was all diamonds. There might have been a couple of rubies thrown in for effect, but it was pretty impressive.

The Kraal dinner was served outside in what I can only describe as a gigantic figure six lying on its side. In the centre was a huge bonfire and then in a ring around the fire were about forty individual tables, set up so everyone was facing the flames. A brilliant design and easy to defend from a swarm of hungry elephants. The food was amazing, the service, perfect and all the lads were jolly.

On the last night, we didn't bother to dress quite so flamboyantly, and I noticed that Bob Halley had discreetly placed a small briefcase under his table.

'What could this be?' I wondered, knowing full well that we had no option but to steal it. Diversionary tactics were employed immediately such as, 'Look at the knob on that monkey up there on the wall,' or, 'My God! Is that a tarantula mating?'

And the deed was done.

We repaired to the bar and settled in for one of the silliest nights I can almost remember. Elton and Rod were on fire. Both very witty and as daft as the contents of a door-to-door salesman's suitcase, we wept with laughter. They both went behind the bar and pretended to be barmaids at one point doing Larry Grayson impressions. Bob was not in attendance.

Meanwhile we had tried to open the briefcase but of course it was very securely locked and so we put it away for the night and at checkout the next morning it was still in our possession. Bob looked a tiny bit flustered but was putting on a brave face.

We waited for the inquisition, but none was forthcoming. He knew how to play this game very well. As we were boarding the little plane, he eventually broke down.

'OK, you bastards. Which one of you has got it?' It seemed only fair to return the briefcase to him and so after only another half an hour of winding him up, we relented and handed it over to him.

'Don't you think you ought to check the contents?' we asked, pretending we were locksmiths on vacation. He opened it up to review an astounding collection of Cartier gems, bracelets, watches, pendants, brooches and rings. Enough for a down payment on a modest rock star's mansion.

'Well darlings,' he purred, 'it all seems to be here.'

'Come on, admit it you were a little bit worried, weren't you?'

'No, not really. After all, it's only Elton's daytime stuff.'

★★★

Malcolm Cullimore was the stage manager for the Rod Stewart Group from 1976 till his death in 1997. Malcolm had scoliosis so badly that he wasn't expected to live past his 10th birthday and, as a consequence of having to prove the medics wrong, he was an extraordinarily determined character. All of 5ft and change, he ran the shows with military precision. Although he was gruff in manner and barked at people from time to time, he was a real softie at heart. He had the bluest, liquid eyes I have ever seen, and they twinkled constantly. We all loved him. When the band was not on the road Malcolm was Rod's personal assistant.

Rod had become mates with Richard Harris, the hell-raising Irish actor who became very famous as much for his offscreen behaviour as for his charismatic stage and screen presence. When Linda and I were accompanying Rod and Alana across the Atlantic on the *QE2* to England, Richard and his wife Ann Turkel came to see us off. Visitors could come on board and party before embarking.

'All ashore that's going ashore,' was heard over the tannoy as departure time drew near. We were having a few glasses of something in Rod's suite and vaguely suggested that Richard and Ann might leave sometime soon. But two Irishmen and a Scot needed to spin a yarn or even nine and suddenly we felt the ship shift. The movement was quite subtle, but the blaring of the ship's foghorn should have alerted us.

'I've got a spare toothbrush,' I suggested to Richard, 'as you seem to be coming to England.'

'Don't worry about it,' he replied with that soft brogue that was his trademark. 'I'll swim back with Ann over me shoulder.'

Fair enough. After all he had played King Arthur and was later to be Dumbledore and so he must know a thing or two. I was much impressed by his nonchalance and we just carried on for at least another hour.

'Rod, why don't you come down to the Bahamas next month? I know you've got some lyrics to write and I'm working on a screenplay. We can write all day and drink all night. Whaddya think?'

'Sounds like a good arrangement,' said the singer. 'But there's just one thing,' he continued. 'I usually travel with my bodyguard who is almost 7ft tall and he requires an especially long bed.'

'No problem,' came the actor's reply. 'I'll have one built for him.'

Then with a yawn and a stretch Richard announces, 'I suppose we'd better clear off as we've dinner with some pals tonight.'

Then I got it. He'd done this before.

The pilot boat ... just on the other side of the Verrazano Bridge a vessel came alongside and Richard and Ann boarded the pilot boat and sailed off.

Cool.

Rod did go eventually to the Bahamas and loved the bemused look on Richard's face when he met them at the airport.

'Where's your 7ft bodyguard?' he inquired, scanning the crowd at arrivals.

'You're lookin' at him,' said Malcolm Cullimore.

★★★

Sometime later, on tour in eastern Europe, Malcolm discovered he was an instrument short …

'Where the hell is the grand piano?' says Malcolm to the local promoter.

The response came in the form of a shrug.

'Have you seen our list of requirements? It's called a rider. The piano is on the rider but it's clearly not on the stage.'

'Er … I don't know …'

Malcolm isn't best pleased. 'Well, if you want a show tonight, you'd better get one, and quickly, as it still has to be tuned. Where were you going to get it from?'

'There's a piano rental place that promised it would deliver a Steinway concert grand, but something's gone horribly wrong and it's Sunday now, so no one is answering.'

'Well … no piano, no gig,' says Malcolm.

The promotor wanders about the stage, which is, by the way, set up in a football stadium. He is scratching his head and cursing under his breath. He stops, suddenly.

'I know where we can get it! The local concert hall has a beautiful one used only for classical music.'

'How are you going to get it here?' asks the ever-practical Malcolm.

'Wrestlers.'

'What?'

'Wrestlers. We'll get wrestlers. My cousin is on the local wrestling team and they can go and get it.'

'And transport?

'Lorry.'

'What kind of lorry?'

'Fruit and veg if you must know. Who cares what kind of lorry?'

'OK, go for it,' says Malcolm, 'but it's on your head.'

So, the wrestlers find the guy with the fruit and veg lorry and drive to the concert hall. After several loud knocks a jobsworth in a dark green apron opens the door.

'We're closed. What's all the racket about and who are you and what do you want?'

'We've come to borrow the piano for a big concert in the football ground. We'll take good care of it and bring it back later tonight.'

'Bugger off, you're not going anywhere with my piano.'

'But we've got money.'

'I don't care what you've got. Clear off before I call the police.'

And with that, the door began to close.

'Hang on, we've got to have it.'

'No bloody way.'

There's a skirmish and, of course, the wrestlers prevail. They collar the jobsworth and pop him into a large closet, jamming the door closed.

'Sorry, we'll let you out later. The rental money is on the table.' Jumping on to the stage and grabbing the piano, they heave it on to the floor, out the door and set it up on the back of the lorry. It's an old beat-up flatbed truck and the gleaming black Steinway sticks out the back.

I remember seeing it coming along the access road as we started our sound check.

'Normally I'd just order pizza to be delivered,' says Malcolm, 'but it's nice to be a little different. Fruit and veg from a … well … a fruit and veg lorry is perfect when you're in trouble.'

'Fruit and veg? That thing sticking out the back doesn't look like any veg I know.'

'I don't know. Use your imagination. From a certain angle it could be a very large aubergine.'

'Now you're being silly. But, in any case, let's get that aubergine on the stage.'

★★★

By now, Rod had moved out of my home, but I had found another housemate, whose tea making wasn't quite up to his efforts, but was a lot prettier than him. Adriana Corajoria was a television presenter. I had met her in New York when my old mate, Federico Gastaldi, now in charge of Fiorucci NY, was invited to a band dinner. He turned up with this beautiful companion. When she left the table, I said to him, 'Your girlfriend is stunning.'

'She's not my girlfriend.'

My spirits lifted. 'How much for her phone number?'

'Nothing to you because you can't afford it,' Federico responded. 'And this isn't 1952. Ask her yourself when she comes back.'

I did, and she gave me her number ... gratis.

Adriana Corajoria was born in Argentina, where her family owned a ranch, and she was a model and aspiring actress. We embarked upon an enormously passionate and happy romance. She moved to LA, signed with model and theatrical agencies and made some television appearances. I was madly in love with her.

We went on holiday to the Greek Island of Zakynthos where I had rented a beach villa for ten days close to a secluded bay. We arrived late one afternoon, full of dreams of white-domed roofs with blue-trimmed windows and small alleys with steep and crooked steps. The idyllic photographs in the brochure had cleverly disguised the fact that years ago the island had suffered a terrible earthquake and the houses had been re-built using grey breeze blocks offering the charm and warmth of a Russian Gulag. The villa owners had forgotten to mention the massive infestation of mosquitos that were living there and not paying any rent. We left the next day, flew to Athens and boarded a hydrofoil at Piraeus bound for the island of Poros. We rented a car and drove off in search of adventure and a comfy bed.

Nothing. Anywhere.

You couldn't sleep on the beach as the police threw anyone off. It was so busy that they put poolside loungers by the dozen on the flat hotel roofs and rented them out. Open air dormitories. Cradle of civilisation? We slept in the car and then found our way to the island of Hydra and stayed in a nice enough hotel on the sand. On the way back to Athens on the boat Adriana and I were seated in the lounge bar relaxing and chatting. A waiter arrived with a large bottle of beer and two glasses.

'Er ... I didn't order this,' I said. 'There's been a mistake.'

'No, no mistake,' came the reply. 'This is from the gentleman over there.' He gestures to an ancient, smiling, Greek gentleman in a suit and tie, who is waving and nodding at us with a lovely, warm look in his eyes. So, we open the beer and gratefully gesture, 'Yamas' or 'Cheers', while wondering what's happening. Eventually a younger man sitting with him comes over and we thank him for the beer, asking whether it is the old gent's birthday or some other celebration.

Now the complications begin because he doesn't speak any English, so between hand gestures, my rusty French, Adriana's perfect Spanish and a word or two of German, the story is pieced together: it appears that the old man lost his son in the war. He was just 18. The son's inseparable best friend from childhood apparently looked exactly like me. Overhearing me speak he knew I couldn't be his son's friend, but it brought back so many cherished memories that he wanted to share them with me by buying us drinks. It was incredibly touching that I should have reminded him of happier times. All those years had passed since his son's death and yet I expect he must have thought of his boy every day.

After we arrived in Piraeus, the two men insisted on finding us a taxi and helped carry our heavy suitcases down the gangplank, even loading them in the car boot. So, with smiles and hugs from perfect strangers, we were on our way. This rare moment of tenderness has stayed with me for more than thirty years and it colours the way I think. And it still encourages me to perform occasional random acts of kindness.

Adriana and I were together for about three years and impressively happy. But I was still very much the rock musician. There was much partying, I was drinking quite a bit and although I was earning lots of money, I was spending too much of it. Adriana was more grounded than me and a bit more mature, which wasn't that difficult in those days. I think she wanted someone who was more stable. She knew I wanted to marry her, but I suppose she thought I was too immature and assumed that I wasn't going to change ... or settle down. When my daughter, Camille was born some years later, I did change my ways almost immediately, but she didn't, of course, know that would happen – after all, neither did I! Adriana decided she'd live on her own for a while and maybe find someone a bit more sensible. Perhaps my boyish charm was beginning to wear a bit thin. However, this break-up hurt like hell.

There were too many memories in the house that we shared together and so I moved to a place just off Sunset. We did manage to remain friends and I unwittingly even played Cupid. I invited Adriana to a party and there she met Miles Copeland, who managed the Police and then Sting. They married in 1989 and my wedding presents were an ironing board to 'iron out life's little wrinkles' for him and a Cartier clock for her. Adriana is a talented sculptress but decided, when her three boys were busy at school, that she would begin to study too. Seven years later she received her doctorate in psychology. Beauty, brains and soul, an irresistible combination.

Rod invited Jeff Beck to join the *Camouflage* tour as he had played on the title track, replacing my guitar parts with his signature sound. I guess if you're going to be taken off the album it's not so bad if it's by Jeff Beck. My style leaned more towards Steve Cropper and the sound I created was generally cleaner and less distorted. I think the producer was right to go for a heavier sound and Jeff's solo was extraordinary. Over a period of four weeks, we met every afternoon rehearsing for the tour. Jeff is a natural player and incredibly inventive. He showed me some things on the guitar that I had always wanted to know how to play – but now thirty years later, I still can't play them. Stuff like playing 16th notes with your thumb in an up and down motion while playing chords with your other fingers.

Jeff was mixing his new album during this period and every day we would ask how it was going. He would reply, 'Just got one more mix and we're done.' Of course, Jeff being such a perfectionist, it still wasn't finished when we left on tour, so sadly he missed out on promoting the album. He seemed a little uncomfortable on the tour – maybe because at one time he had been Rod's boss, when Rod was the singer in the Jeff Beck band and Ronnie Wood played bass. It was nice having him around, and he played with us for about five shows. Then, one day, he just wasn't there on the plane. In typical fashion we'd heard that he'd gone home because, in his words, 'My pet duck is sick.'

One of the unfair advantages of being associated with a famous singer is that people want to be nice to you. I always thought it was a good idea to let them. In this case, we somehow made friends with a young guy called Martin (not his real name) who was the youngest skipper of the largest yacht in Marina Del Rey. *The Greek Tycoon* was available for charter and that's how we met. With my love of boats, I soon found myself getting invited to sunset cruises because as Martin explained, 'The owner realises that every week, I need to take the boat out past the three-mile limit to empty the tanks.'

Nice. That gave Martin tacit permission to throw a small party every week. He was a handsome young man, probably about 25 and, as he lived aboard ship, he knew lots of people in the marina. Some of them were girls. Some of them could easily be described as attractive. So, let's see: free yacht party, rock musicians, attractive girls, Pacific Ocean. I'm beginning to wonder why I ever left California.

I was about to reach the incredibly old age of 40 and to help me celebrate, my mother and father came over from England. Martin suggested that we have the party on *The Greek Tycoon*. Rod and all the boys in the band were invited plus the guys from the Record Plant, the infamous Los Angeles studio, where we were recording. It was going very well. We had cruised up and down the main channel, as it was too rough to go past the breakwater. There were about eighty people on board, some of them had climbed up on to the roof of the flying bridge, where all the radar and antenna were located. Uh-oh ... my dear American friend Kevin Eddy, an engineer at the studio, was sitting next to the revolving radar scanner when somebody switched it on. This massive piece of metal caught him in the face and it broke off his front teeth.

We immediately returned to the dock and called the paramedics who whisked him off to hospital, but my enduring memory was that Kevin was so heavily anaesthetised by that potent cocktail of cocaine and cognac, that he hardly felt the thing. He held a blood-soaked towel to his face and smiled. Dear God, the damage was quite shocking.

'Sorry to mess up the party,' he said, 'but I think I should get this looked at.'

And I thought the British were good at understatement. The paramedics took him away. We all went home. A few days later he was back at the studio with a new set of gnashers as if nothing had happened. I have always been grateful to him for not calling the lawyers and suing the pants and other items of clothing off me and Martin. Thanks Kevin.

While Plum and Age were here, we asked Martin if we could go down to Long Beach Harbour for the afternoon. So off we went. It was a beautiful day but that is no surprise around there. The harbour is a proper working port with freighters, tankers and all sorts coming and going. You really do you have to keep your wits about you so with this in mind I naturally thought Plum ought to take the wheel.

'Oh no, I couldn't,' she says, edging towards the door of the bridge.

'Oh, come on Plum, its easy, just like driving a car.'

'But I don't drive.'

'Well, think of it more like a pony and trap.'

'Clear off the lot of you. It's a 100ft yacht, no sign of a donkey, unless I count you,' she said fixing me with a steely glare.

'Look, Plum, it's easy,' I added nonchalantly, leading her to the wheel and standing behind her, placing her hands on the wheel. 'Look, there's nothing about, except that tanker and it's miles away.'

'Dear God, Jimmy, what are you getting me into?'

'You'll be fine,' I encouraged, stepping back a fraction to leave her in control. Swiftly I bolted out the door and disappeared from view.

'JIMMY!' she yelled. 'Get back here now!'

'I've just got to go to the loo, Plum. Won't be a moment.'

'ARGHHH ...'

What a rotten son I turned out to be.

Of course, she didn't know that the skipper was up on the flybridge, with a duplicate set of controls so she was never in any danger. I think she realised everything was OK when, to avoid the oncoming tanker, the wheel miraculously turned itself. After a large gin and tonic, she saw the funny side of it. Sometimes these things have just got to be done.

We seemed to be out on the water quite a lot in the Stewart band. At any opportunity we would beg borrow or steal a boat, even if it was only for a pirates' day out. On one occasion we were in Sydney Harbour on a large motor yacht that had probably been chartered by the promotor, Paul Dainty. We were heading for the beach with the idea of swimming a bit and maybe a cold beer.

We dropped anchor just outside the shark nets, by a beautiful beach. I was dressed in only my swimsuit, a T-shirt and my new Ray Ban sunglasses. Peering over the side, I wanted to see how deep it was by looking down the anchor chain to the bottom. Shadows flitted around outside the nets which could just have been anything. Any kind of fish. Or anything oceanic. Well, of course, Kevin Savigar, me old mate, couldn't resist the temptation and flipped me over the side. Lazily tumbling down the 12 or more feet to the water. My life in slow motion.

Someone called out, 'No, no, no! Shark-infested waters!'

This was followed immediately by Rod calling out, 'Anyone got Ron Wood's phone number?'

My Olympic sprint to the stern of the yacht obviously outstripped any old tiger shark in the neighbourhood and, panting a bit, I climbed the swim ladder to the afterdeck.

'You OK?' asked the singer with a hint of a smile.

'Yeah,' I replied. 'I just thought I was gonna lose my new sunglasses.'

'I'm glad you're all right 'cos no one's got Woody's number anyway.'

Rod and I had quite a history with boats. On a whim he bought a very fast Italian boat called a Riva 2000. I once had a Rover 2000 but that's not really relevant, so I'm not sure why I mentioned it. This thing had three, yes three, overblown V8 Chevy 454 engines and was unbearably fast at about 70mph.

We never had it flat out. As I was once in the 1st Lilliput Sea Scouts I was obviously fully qualified to drive this beast. Like a 5-year-old in a Ferrari.

After a couple of trips with a skipper I was deemed capable of taking it out on my own. I always went with another person, but I was essentially the infant in charge. Rod, Kelly Emberg and I went over to Catalina in the Riva one afternoon, hung around the Isthmus and then had dinner. However, getting ready to return to Marina Del Rey, we encountered a couple of problems. Firstly, the engines wouldn't start and then, when we somehow managed to get them going, the navigation lights wouldn't come on.

The stretch of ocean between Long Beach and Catalina is pretty busy. Oil tankers, freighters, cruise ships and fishermen all come out to play. I had completed a few night crossings in sailboats and you really needed to pay attention.

We deliberated for a while about staying the night, but the Isthmus has no hotel and it's quite a way to walk to Avalon in high heels – even if we could find a hotel anyway. In retrospect, I suppose Rod could have ditched the high heels.

'Let's risk it,' Kelly said.

'...OK, but we need to keep a sharp lookout,' I replied, suddenly all grown-up. The Riva only works properly at speed, when you get it up on a plane, so you need to do about 25 miles an hour or so. It was a pretty uneventful crossing, but as we neared the entrance to the Marina a 'Big Black Thing' thundered out of the darkness. It was about the size of a delivery van.

We whizzed past it. It hadn't any lights either.

'Arghhh! What was that!' I yelled. 'Where the hell did that come from?'

It hit me like a Titanic iceberg; we were in the oil tanker mooring area and these were their mooring buoys. They are big, tough, steel barrels, chained to the sea bed and only movable with kryptonite. The buoys are marked on a chart, which of course we didn't have. They would also have shown up on radar – but we didn't have that either. We were on the futuristic, high-speed equivalent of the *Kon Tiki* raft. But with a toilet. And suede walls. More shaken than one of James Bond's Martinis, we crept back to the marina leaving unspoken the thoughts of the carnage that might have happened.

Lucky.

We had another near nautical disaster when one bright spark once suggested that we go out in the Riva for couple of hours.

'I'll call the skipper,' says Rod, 'and we'll grab a few beers and get going.'

Kevin Savigar, Rod and I join Nigel, the skipper and a twenty-four flat-pack of beer and away we go. We'd been in the studio a lot and a break on the ocean is always good to clear the mind. We had tried putting on our dive masks and snorkels without going to the beach, but it didn't have the same effect. We tried this driving down

La Cienega Boulevard in Kev's classic convertible Mustang, pouring beer down each other's snorkels like upside-down hosepipes, but the beer tasted of rubber.

'The boat doesn't seem to be going too well, Nigel,' says Rod.

'Yes, it's a little sluggish,' comes the reply.

'I'll nip below and get more beer,' says Kev. 'It's probably all that weight in the front, slowing us down.'

'I'll go,' says I.

'No, let me,' says Rod.

'No, I'll do it,' insists Kev.

This is a band routine where everyone volunteers, but no one moves.

'You'd better have look at this,' says Nigel, his head sticking up from the companionway.

Gasp! Shock! Horror!

'Hmmm, we seem to be sinking, Nigel. Life jackets? Life raft? Kitchen sink?'

'Don't mention sink.'

The cabin has about a foot of water in it and the perfect suede interior is all messed up.

'I'll grab the beer,' says Kev, being quite sensible. So, we settled down on the banquette while Nigel called the coastguard.

'I suppose we'd better head back then,' I suggested. We were only about half an hour away from the marina.

'Coastguard Marina del Rey here. What's the name of your vessel?' the voice crackled nicely.

'*Cruel But Fair*,' we chorused.

'Seems appropriate,' he muttered.

But they couldn't have been nicer. We crept back and just made it to the coastguard dock.

'You guys are very lucky,' says a young officer. 'Another ten minutes and you'd have been on the bottom.' They put three or four portable pumps into the Riva and it gradually started to empty. We sat on the dock, enjoying the sun and finishing the beer. The pumps sprayed the water into the air and made rainbows.

A perfect day out.

★★★

The biggest crowd I ever played for was an estimated 350,000 people, at the inaugural Rock in Rio festival, which lasted for ten days. The event also featured Queen, James Taylor, AC/DC and Yes, among others. We were booked to headline twice – on the second day and about a week later. So, we were stuck in Rio for the duration. Kicking our heels. Not.

We stayed at the Copacabana Beach hotel with some of the other musicians, including the Go-Go's – a petite, punkish group from LA, who had reached number one in the US album charts (the first all women band to do so). More importantly, they were very friendly, pretty rowdy, and great fun. I knew their bassist, Kathy Valentine, and one night, both our bands had the night off.

We went out to dinner at Maxim's, which had absolutely nothing in common with the legendary Parisian restaurant, apart from a shared name.

The restaurant was quite formal and classy – unlike the food which was neither. However, that could have been because we had already absorbed huge quantities of Peruvian marching powder prior to leaving the hotel. I suspect we had a paternal attitude towards the girls – they were out with the big boys and we ought to take care of them, but we soon discovered that the girls could certainly take care of themselves and certainly hold their own in our company.

We pushed the food around the plates for an hour or two and then headed off to the hotel bar, drinking until closing time. We went back to somebody's room and with the assistance of more stimulants, continued carousing into the morning. At about 11 a.m., I said goodbye to Rod, Robin, Kevin and the girls as we were playing later that night.

'Meet you all in the bar at nine tonight.'

'Nine o'clock? What time are you guys on?'

'11 p.m.,' I replied before staggering to my room.

I heard later that the party finally wrapped up around two in the afternoon after a swim on Copacabana beach – most likely with everyone fully clothed. At nine, somewhat shaky, I entered the bar, half expecting that the girls would have bailed. But ... no, they were still knocking them back as if nothing had happened.

'Hi girls, what time did you finish?'

'Finish? We haven't been to bed yet. Here have a Cuba Libre, they are very good.'

'Not bloody likely, I've got to play tonight.'

'What? Call yourselves rock and rollers? You guys turned out to be a bunch of pussies.'

So, with the band's reputation at stake, I knocked back a cocktail or two – just enough to loosen me up for the show that night. I never drink much before the show. Despite all the shenanigans backstage, we were always very professional onstage.

The experience of performing to such a huge crowd was quite something. I remember looking out from the stage at the enormous numbers of people and thinking this is unreal. The stage was quite high and being at night, the floodlights illuminated the audience, so we could see quite a way back, but I still couldn't see where the audience actually ended. It was incredibly exhilarating, and you couldn't help but feel a huge buzz of energy, appearing in front of so many people. But, funnily enough, it didn't make me feel nervous. The audience were on our side – they hadn't, after all, paid all that money to see you, have a rotten time and throw things at you. They wanted to enjoy themselves. An event like that is obviously much more impersonal than playing in smaller clubs, which can actually be scarier because the audience can almost hear you breathe.

Somewhere along the line, Rod had a brief fling with *Woman in Red* actress Kelly LeBrock. He found her – as we all did, funny, wild and sexy. She invited Rod and me to her house for dinner and with a few other guests we sat at a very low table eating Lebanese style with our fingers. Kelly was wearing a djellaba, a sort of unisex robe from the Middle East, and nothing else. She would lean over the table to serve us with the whole front of her garment revealing everything. Of course, I was delighted. Rod wasn't quite so delighted in my delight.

Some months later, Kelly decided to marry action hero Steven Seagal, much approved by no one. He had called me up one time when he wanted me to play in a band he was putting together. While we were talking, someone else rang me and I put him on hold. When I came back to him, he had hung up and never contacted me again.

Kelly then asked me to be in a band to play at their wedding reception, which was to take place in the basement of a restaurant in Beverly Hills. It was quite a band and included Jackson Browne, Lamont Dozier on vocals, Phil Chen on bass and Ian Wallace on drums. I was particularly knocked out to be on stage with Lamont Dozier, who had written some of the greatest ever Motown hits, which we got to play that night. Lamont was gentle, delightful and sang like an angel. And there was Jackson Browne ... a perfectionist who was a bad choice for this kind of gig. He thought we were his band and he should tell us what and how to play. We had learned the songs and interpreted them in our own way, but he wanted us to recreate the songs on his records. We weren't a cover group. He was as much fun as a nail through your foot. Nevertheless, we still had a great time and Kelly was adorable.

The last time I saw her was at a rodeo near Bernie Taupin's ranch. She had escaped Seagal and was happy to be free again. But it was very sad to see the relationship had taken its toll on her and the carefree girl I once knew was now subdued. I think things are much better for Kelly now. She has since remarried and devotes her time to charities supporting terminally ill children whereas Seagal was recently appointed as a special envoy for Russia by President Vladimir Putin.

You can probably work out why they weren't suited ...

7

A Bird Never Flew on One Wing

Man does not control his own fate. The women in his life do that for him.

Groucho Marx

The year of 1987 turned out to be a very significant year for me – particularly when it came to my personal and professional relationship with Rod. In the middle of June, he called me. I knew something was up, although it wasn't me. It was 8.30 a.m. on a Sunday – very early in rock and roll terms. In fact, I knew exactly why he was calling.

'Hey pal. What's up? How's Emberg?' (I always called Kelly Emberg – I forget why.)

'She's great. And Ruby is gorgeous. Born last night. Sorry to wake you.'

'That's OK. Congrats!'

'Thanks. Can you do something for me?'

'Sure.'

'We're starving hungry, Kelly's been awake all night – we can't get any food. Could you make us some bacon sandwiches and bring them down to the hospital?'

'Of course. Give me two minutes.'

I fried the bacon, buttered the bread, wrapped the sandwiches in paper napkins and put them in a brown paper bag. I nipped down the hill to the maternity wing of the Cedars-Sinai hospital. It was now after 9 a.m. and the place was bustling. The delicious smell of the bacon wafted up from the paper bag. I hadn't had time for breakfast. My mouth was watering and I was tempted to just take one bite. No, that wouldn't do. I was on a mission.

As soon as I entered the maternity wing, I seemed to attract an undue amount of attention. There seemed to be a lot of people looking at me. There was much pointing. Heads swivelled and shook with shock. Jaws dropped. Eyebrows furrowed as the scent of fried bacon wafted through the corridors. I increased my pace, fearful of attack.

I blustered my way into Kelly's room.

'What's that you got there?'

'Never you mind, just pass me that sandwich,' replied an exhausted but beautiful Emberg.

I handed over the goods. Rod happily tucked in whilst giving me a very knowing look.

'I tried several delis before I called you, but no one else in their right mind would deliver bacon sandwiches here. You'd better take the back way out.'

Ah. I'd been walking through Cedars-Sinai hospital, one of Los Angeles' most famous Jewish institutions, reeking of bacon. No wonder I was getting the kosher stares.

I was honoured to be asked to be godfather to Ruby. In fact, it was Kelly who had asked me to undertake this sacred task. Over thirty years later, Ruby and I continue to have a lovely, easy-going relationship and I have written a couple of songs with her. My son Mackenzie has also worked with Ruby and Rod and I have amused ourselves wondering if our offspring might one day be in a band together. In fact, Ruby is in a great band with country singer and songwriter Alyssa Bonagura called the Sisterhood.

That same year, I wrote what I consider to be one of my favourite compositions. We were in the studio, but it wasn't going well. Rod announced, 'I'm going to take a break. This track's not working out. I'm going shopping.'

As he left, I suggested to Kevin Savigar, 'Well, he either needs a pair of socks or another Lamborghini.'

Kevin nodded stoically, 'Too early to go to the pub?'

'Yes, just a bit,' I replied reluctantly. 'It would be nice if we could come up with something so the whole day hasn't been wasted.'

Kevin, equally reluctant, agreed. I continued, 'I've got this bit of an idea that I wrote on the new guitar synth that I've just bought.'

'Let's have an earhole.'

I played the verse and sang the melody of the song.

'Could be a bit like U2.'

'Yes, I can see that,' I said hopefully.

We ran it a couple of times. Kevin was now on top form. 'I know. How about if we try this?'

Out popped the chorus.

'Yes, that seems to work. Nice.'

'What about a bridge?'

'This might work,' I replied. And somehow quite easily the song was completed – all bar the lyrics.

We continued to work on it until Rod returned.

'So, lads, got anything?'

'Yeah, give this a try.'

We played the song and Rod started to add his own ideas to it, until musically it was all there.

'Let's put it down.'

But, later in the studio, when we came to overdub more instruments on the track, Rod was undecided and suggested it might not make the album. My heart sank. Not only did I really like this song but losing a co-writing credit would certainly impact my supply of beer vouchers. There was this moment of stunned silence. Then, to my everlasting gratitude, the recording engineer, Steve MacMillan, who almost never offered an opinion or commented in any way about what was going on, slowly turned away from the console and looked directly at Rod.

'I wouldn't do that if I were you. This is the best song you've got.'

Swiftly recovering from the shock of hearing a remark from Steve, Rod responded with a smile.

'If that's the case, then I suppose we'd better get on with it.'

As I have probably already mentioned, to succeed, you really have to be lucky.

That song became 'Forever Young'. There were some similarities to the Bob Dylan song of the same name. But consciously or unconsciously, Rod had used two lines from Bob's song. After it was released we heard from his publishers that we were in breach and Bob claimed the whole lyric and the royalties. This was a real shame because Rod had come up with some brilliant stuff of his own and if he only hadn't used those two lines …

At least I can say I got to co-write with Bob Dylan. And as co-author of the music my royalties were untouched. The song was one of the most successful songs we recorded at that time, went on to enjoy virtual anthem status in America and Rod was nominated for a Grammy for the vocal performance.

Looking back, it seems particularly untimely and somewhat ironic that I was to leave the band so soon after the success of 'Forever Young'. Rod decided to replace Tony Brock with another Tony – Tony Thompson, a session musician and Chic's former drummer. I'm not sure why as we all thought Tony Brock was brilliant. I wasn't privy to these discussions, but heard about it from Rod's manager, who subsequently decided Tony Thompson would become co-band leader with me. My immediate reaction was very negative. It was quite difficult to cue the band from the drums and we would have to turn away from the audience to watch for the signals.

In retrospect, I feel management's opinion was that I had become too influential. And they knew what was best for Rod. They didn't want to fire me, but they certainly wanted to clip my wings. I wasn't having any of it. The lack of respect from the management to the band was apparent. Like a lot of people who don't have any real experience of the dynamic created between artists and musicians, they see us as easily replaceable. So, I quit.

I wrote a heartfelt letter to Rod, explaining I couldn't work under his management regime and I needed to move on. The two of us met for dinner at one of our favourite restaurants, Le Dôme on Sunset Strip – a great place for musicians to hang out as the owner, Eddie Kerkhofs, would take guests any time of the night. We had enjoyed numerous 'lockdowns' there over the years. But that night we shared a sad and pretty emotional evening. I believe Rod's management had persuaded him that it would be for the best if I wasn't in the band any longer and he shouldn't try to persuade me otherwise. I was out of the band and they subsequently hired a guitar player who looked great in a pair of leather trousers – his best attribute. Tony Thompson didn't last long either. It was a sudden and dramatic turn of events and the end of an era for me.

In the meantime, my older brother Maurice had managed to move as far away from me as possible. He lived in the United Arab Emirates and I still lived in Los Angeles. We were twelve time zones apart which reminds me about a gift I bought my sister Joyce when she said she needed a clock with two time zones on it. This was so she could communicate with her eldest son Henry, who lived in New Zealand. As she unwrapped the present and we checked the local time in Auckland we realised it was a twelve-hour time difference, so both clock faces were identical. Well, we are Irish.

So, it was a rare occasion that Maurice and I were both in England. When this does happen, tradition has it that my father, Maurice and I would sit up and set the world to rights over a bottle of whisky. With much ceremony, the 'Aged One' went to the kitchen and returned with a shabby old silver tray, a small jug of water, three Waterford glass whisky tumblers and a new bottle of single malt. Setting it down on the table, he deftly unscrewed the top and with an accuracy rivalled only by Kobe Bryant, tossed it into the wastepaper basket.

'Well we won't be needing that,' says he with a determined look.

'So, boys, what in the world have you been up to?'

And so, it began: stories of broken romances, major screw-ups and shenanigans of the first order. We had a lot of catching up to do. At about midnight, whilst in full flight, there was a loud banging on the ceiling coming from the bedroom above.

'Age! What the hell is that?'

'Hang on a minute, it's just your mother. I'll see what she wants.'

He opens the door from the living room and is about to call up the stairs.

Before he can say a word, we hear Plum.

'Bob! Have you not had enough yet? Isn't it time for bed?'

'Ah, we'll just be a few more minutes,' he responds, eyeing the whisky and noticing that there was still a third of the bottle left. 'Go back to sleep, I'll be up in a minute,' he calls, lying through his dentures.

It turned out that Plum had an old blackthorn, silver-topped walking stick that she kept beside the bed for the sole purpose of indicating to her husband that it was bedtime. It is only just crossing my mind now that perhaps Age had similar traditions with other members of the family. Anyway, we carried on until the second barrage announced the mother was still awake and getting grumpier.

'Let's get her down here,' suggested Maurice, eliciting a flash of the 'Kelly Eye' from Dad. This particular look that Age had perfected could melt granite at a hundred paces. Fortunately, Maurice was looking the other way although the back of his neck was slightly singed.

'That's a good idea,' I said, with whisky-filled courage. 'I'll go up and get her.'

My favourite 1964 Stratocaster in 1978.

One of the 'Young Turks', *Camouflage* tour, 1984.

With Adriana and Rod – 'Do ya think we're sexy?'

Early doors with Adriana. One of us was a model.

Got this off Elvis when he wasn't looking.

Farm Dogs version 1 – a shady bunch. Left to right: Dennis Tufano, Tony Brock, Me, Pete Buckland, Bernie Taupin and Robin Le Mesurier.

The name's Cregan. James Cregan.

Celts in kilts

Mackenzie showing me a chord.

On stage with Katie Melua – 'Pure Voice; Pure Heart'.

The force of nature that is Ava.

Cockney Rebel reunion. Left to right: Mona Wagner, Stuart Elliot, Me, Steve Harley, Barry Wickens and Lisa Wagner.

Silly night out in January 2019. Left to right: Ronnie and Sally Wood, Penny and Rod Stewart, and some old bloke.

Unexpectedly unavailable. My current band, Cregan & Co. Left to right: Sam Tanner, Ben Mills, Harry James, Jim Cregan, Pat Davey. *(Steve Crispe)*

JC 2019. *(Peter Zownir Photography)*

Much love and shenanigans with the Cregan/Samson Clan.

'Come on, Mum, you never sit up with us. Come down and just have one drink. Then we'll all go to bed.'

'All right, just this once. I'll be down in a minute, please just make me a gin and tonic.'

A few minutes later she arrives wearing one of those floral house-coats, slightly quilted and somewhat past its prime. We were all relieved to see that she had left the walking stick upstairs. Her only weapon was a fierce sense of morality and an Irish countrywoman's instinctive defence against the dark arts. We boys were slightly stymied by the arrival of one so virtuous in our midst, so the conversation lagged until Maurice turned it to swearing.

'You know Plum, in all my 45 years I have never heard you say a swear word or anything mildly vulgar. That's quite a record. We were wondering (it seems that Age and I are also now involved) if just once, you would say the worst possible swear words that you know.'

'Ahh Maurice, you are a bold, bold boy. How could you even dream of asking your mother such a thing?'

'Oh, go on Mum,' says I, feeling safety in numbers. 'I promise we will never ever ask you again.'

'Whissht … away with you,' came the quick reply. Plum was not much of a drinker and initially she refused another drink, but under my 'guidance' and getting her to admit that this was a special occasion, she agreed with the mischievous. 'Oh well I suppose. A bird never flew on one wing.'

Having boys in her house again, she was not averse to letting her hair down a bit. Of course, it couldn't be let down very far as she was still wearing her night-time rollers. She had maintained the same hairstyle from the 1930s. It was her badge of honour.

The conversation wandered off into the other realms until once again the subject of bad language was broached.

'Look, Mum, we will never ask you this again but just this once, say the worst thing you know. You can whisper it if you like and we will never tell anyone that you did this.'

'Oh, all right, anything to stop you keeping on at me.'

We leaned in closer, so as not to miss anything.

'Bloody bugger,' she whispered.

'What was that?'

'Bloody bugger!'

We fell about laughing but Plum cannily got her way as we all went off to bed.

And of course, the bottle was empty.

This was one of the last occasions that we were all together. The Cregans excel in family reunions and one unforgettable gathering took place in Dublin during the *Foolish Behaviour* tour, in late 1980. My stipulation was that I would invite and pay for anyone who was connected to the family in any way, no matter how indeterminate. No one argued. My cousin Rory was president of the very prestigious Irish Law Society and he arranged for us to use its HQ, Blackhall Place, a former hospital and described as 'one of the most beautiful and, in its way, original' of Dublin's major buildings.

Hugh, Rory's brother, who later became a judge and with whom I am very close, embraced the whole idea of a rock musician in the family. How incongruous that my brother Maurice was a captain in the British Army, three cousins, all brothers, were lawyers and most of my relatives were pillars of the establishment. Then there was me.

A full Christmas dinner was planned – but before we sat down to a typical tablecreaker, we had all gathered with the band members for reasons I forget, at the bar for a few snifters. Mother was so happy, but had just confessed that, to make the occasion perfect, Maurice and his wife Judy should be also be there. As luck would have it, this was the very moment that Maurice and Judy appeared in the doorway. Unbeknownst to Mum, I had arranged for them to fly in secretly from Dubai. We gave them a rousing cheer and burst into applause as they crossed the floor to give Mum and Dad a hug. At first Mum didn't know what was happening but was then overcome with joy. I'll never forget the look on her face. The whole bar was in tears at her reaction.

It was normal in my family to have a party piece, so the children sang and danced, Maurice recited some verse that he had written about my father – an elegiac, sensitive, poem, entitled 'Age and the stripper'. We sang and danced and hugged and cried until the early hours.

Seven years later, the tears flowed again for Mum, but not tears of joy. She had been unwell for a long time with leukaemia and was becoming very frail. I had been going back and forth from LA to visit, witnessing her slow decline. I then received a call, asking me if I'd go on tour to Germany with singer Jennifer Rush, who was a huge star there and promoting her latest album, *Heart Over Mind*. I arrived for two weeks of rehearsals in Munich with a lot of people I didn't know other than ex-wife Linda's sister Shirley, who was one of the backing singers. Before starting rehearsals, I stopped for a couple of days in the UK and managed to see Mum. It turned out to be for the last time.

A few days later, while I was back in Munich, she passed away. She was only 72 and, as I write this, the same age as me. I told Jennifer, who was wonderfully understanding and considerate in giving me her blessing to leave the tour temporarily to return to the UK for the funeral. The ceremony took place in Christchurch, Dorset where Mum and Dad had been living and, to be honest, I can't remember much about it. I have blotted it out from my memory, so painful was it. Although, of course, desperately sad, I guess we were all relieved that she was no longer suffering. I suppose this is a common feeling for all relatives – witnessing the last few weeks or months of a terminal illness is a terrible ordeal for the patient and everyone connected. I am convinced that it would be much more humane if the laws of assisted suicide in the UK were changed.

I returned to the tour terribly upset, desperately sad, and a little under-rehearsed. I think the loss of my mother, who was the first person close to me to pass away, helped me understand what Robin Le Mesurier had also been through when his mother Hattie Jacques had passed away. Several years later, Robin received the news that his musician brother Jake, aged 35, had died from a heroin overdose in Barcelona. As soon as I heard about Jake, I insisted that I spend time with Robin. I didn't want him to be alone, depressed and drinking. He is a lovely guy, but it's fair to say he is terribly English when it comes to sharing his emotions.

But, on this occasion, Robin was more open about his brother. I thought being at the beach would be therapeutic and so we drove down Mulholland Drive to the Pacific Ocean. We passed the day there while Robin reminisced about Jake. There were tears, but also laughs as Robin described some of his brother's more eccentric behaviour over the years.

In 1990 Robin played on an album I recorded at the Cherokee studios in West Hollywood. I had been writing and producing for the London Quireboys, a rock band who had aspirations of being the 1990s equivalent of the Faces. Managed by Sharon Osborne, they were a hard-drinking, drug-taking bunch of lunatics, but surprisingly clever. Strangely enough, guitarist Guy Bailey and the piano player, Chris Johnstone, would do *The Times* cryptic crossword every afternoon before we got down to work in the studio.

The album, *Little Bit of What You Fancy*, was fun to make but I had to do lots of 'repairing', occasionally using other musicians to tighten up the performance. Unfortunately, the first thing I had to do at the end of day one was to fire the drummer. He just wasn't ready to make the record and I explained that he should keep practising, stay with the band, and that he would be OK. I cited Ringo Starr as an example, but unfortunately the drummer's ego got the better of him (a well-worn phrase) and he quit.

I brought in Ian Wallace, who had worked with Bob Dylan, Ry Cooder and Crosby, Stills and Nash among others and was magnificent. Without a great drummer, you can't make a great rock record. The album was a hit in the UK and in the end had some chart success, including going platinum in Canada, but as luck would have it the Black Crows (the band that cornered the market that the Faces had left empty) released an album six weeks before ours came out and completely eclipsed our record. We were considered 'also rans' even though we were making the records at the same time and knew nothing about their endeavours.

Unfortunately, when it was time to make the second album (*Bitter Sweet & Twisted*), the management approached Bob Rock, the Canadian producer who commanded a fee of $150,000 – three times what I had received. He hadn't, however, been aware how much additional work I had done after the band had left the studio. It was rumoured that his first effort was rejected by EMI records and Rolling Stone producer Chris Kimsey was brought in for further doctoring. It was disappointing to be replaced as I felt that I had done a pretty good job and even more so, that I didn't get another job from EMI, despite the success of the Quireboys' first album.

There was, however, a silver lining to the whole experience. A very attractive silver lining. In those days, bands recorded live in the studio, so we used to have lots of visitors, which often made the sessions much more sociable and enjoyable. One such visitor, Jane Booke, was a friend of the engineer, George Tutko, and turned up one day at the studio to watch some of the recording. She was bright, funny, sexy. Three of my favourite adjectives. I was single and so was she. We started dating.

Jane came from wealthy stock, had grown up in Bel Air and had led a fairly solitary life while her mother and stepfather travelled extensively collecting orchids and pre-Columbian art, as one does. They had amassed huge private collections of both. Jane had studied acting at the Lee Strasberg Institute in Hollywood and had been cast in a few films and television but had now turned her attention to music.

I agreed to produce some demos for her. I said I could get a band together at Cherokee studios and with George's help, we'd cut a couple of tracks. Everyone was happy with the arrangement, except the drummer in her band, whose name I can't recall. I can recall, however, that unlike the rest of the musicians, who were doing this as a favour, he insisted on being paid as well as having a list of personal demands. He wanted an endless supply of Evian water, new drumsticks, and a limo to take him to the studio. I'm surprised he didn't ask for a personal masseuse and an evening with Raquel Welch.

I tried to reason with him for about thirty seconds, but he refused to back down and so I got rid of him. I called in an old friend of mine to help out; the Pretenders' Martin Chambers. Not a bad dep. The original drummer changed his mind and asked me to reconsider, but it was too late ... and I think we were somehow better off with Martin in the band!

The demos were OK, but to be honest Jane wasn't the strongest singer and she had also recently lost out on an acting job to Debbie Harry and so sensibly decided on a career outside the entertainment industry as a highly regarded clothes and perfume designer.

Jane had a lovely cottage, high up in the Hollywood Hills – much nicer than mine – so I got rid of my house and moved in with her. We lived up Laurel Canyon near the top of Lookout Mountain Drive and although we didn't have a city view, we looked over beautiful wooded hillsides. It was a pretty idyllic time – I was producing and writing and Jane and I were very happy. Although she didn't drink, Jane embraced the lifestyle which included lots of gatherings and dinner parties. But I behaved myself. It was time for me to settle down. Jane became pregnant and we married in 1990.

Rod lent us his home for the wedding reception. All my family came over and I have to say it was wonderful. We rode in a London double decker bus from church to Rod's where champagne was served on the lawn, followed by a huge buffet in the grand ballroom, housing 100 people. Rod was a great host. There was no seating plan, except for the wedding party and he made sure everyone was seated before discovering there was no place for him! We finally found a table and then the lights all fused, and we were thrown into darkness – much to the delight of the guests. Complete chaos and utter madness.

That night Jane and I took a limo to Santa Barbara and stayed in the Biltmore. The family joined us a few days later, but we couldn't have an extended honeymoon as I was in the middle of making a record.

My gorgeous daughter Camille was born on 3 January 1991 in the very same maternity wing of the Cedars-Sinai, the scene of the bacon sandwich fiasco some years before. I was delighted to be present at the birth and relieved that I hadn't been banned by the hospital staff. The medics had discovered that she had the birth cord around her neck and so Jane, after trying to deliver naturally, had to undergo an emergency 'C' section.

Camille was slightly jaundiced and placed in an incubator. Our doctor, paediatrician to the stars – all Gucci and cashmere – removed Camille from the special care unit and brought her back to Jane shortly after birth. But Camille's condition deteriorated and her jaundice was more noticeable. Concerned, I tried to telephone the doctor, but couldn't get hold of him and he didn't return my calls. Jane and I became very anxious and we agreed, whatever the doctor said, to return Camille to the safety of her incubator. She remained for a week, while on a drip, before we took her home. In the meantime, I had fired 'Dr Cool'.

When I first held Camille in my arms, it was as if a secret hidden door in my heart opened and, in an instant, I was given the gift of a completely new kind of love. That of fatherhood. One that would never fade. One that would continue to grow with time and one that would transform me forever. One of life's greatest blessings. And soon after she was born, I gave myself a good talking to.

'You're a dad now, behave yourself.'

I stopped dabbling in cocaine and smoking and kept my Martinis to a minimum. I wanted to be a good dad. It's funny how, like many men, you worry about what kind of dad you are going to be or even if you're cut out for this kind of commitment. Being a parent was the best thing I'd ever done and changing my lifestyle was necessary. I'm still alive.

The joy of Camille's birth was tempered by my father's death the following year. He had been living alone since he had been widowed, but eventually moved in with my sister Joyce and her husband, Robert, who had both been looking after him steadfastly for about six months. I'm so lucky to be part of such a devoted and loving family.

My dad was admitted to hospital and I returned from LA to be with him and the family. We had been grumpy about how he had been treated while hospitalised. Although he had received the treatment he needed, he had smoked all his life and, no matter how much we pleaded, the medics wouldn't give him a nicotine patch, which would have given him some comfort. We were all gathered at Joyce and Robert's house one night when we had a call from the hospital that he had passed away.

Before the funeral, Dad had an open casket at the funeral home and I went to say goodbye, which turned out to be a big mistake. He had been the subject of a brain autopsy and the invasive procedure had made him look like someone completely different from the man I knew and loved. That image stays with me to this day.

Nothing prepares you for bereavement and mourning. No one can teach you how to grieve. You think you should know how to behave, but we learn from other people and, of course, everyone's experience is deeply personal. You don't know what you're going to be like. I thought of all the books and movie scenes in which death was depicted. But these weren't real. This was real life – or should I say death. I thought back to my mother's death and felt guilty that I hadn't really wept for her.

Some months later, I was descending the stairs leading to the street from my front door. Two thirds of the way down, my legs buckled from under me and I collapsed on the steps and wept uncontrollably for what seemed like an age. I felt I had been sandbagged. It was as if I'd held on to the pain for all this time and it finally had to be released. This was absolute and pure, unadulterated grief. I was no longer playing the role of a bereaved son. This was authentic … and cathartic. I didn't know I had it in me. One of my favourite books is *Love in the Time of Cholera* by Gabriel García Márquez and this quote summed up the loss I was feeling at the time: 'Perhaps this is what the stories meant when they called somebody heartsick. Your heart and your stomach and your whole insides felt empty and hollow and aching.'

8

Nobody Knows Anything

Everybody has a heart. Except some people.

Eve Harrington (Bette Davis)
All About Eve

The Grammy Awards – usually held at the Greek Theatre in Griffith Park – typified much of the shallowness of LA life. For a start, everyone hired a limousine – it was not only expected, it was probably enforceable by law. The difficulty was the meet afterwards as there were over 2,000 limos queuing from the Greek to somewhere east of Timbuctoo. Pre-mobile phones, you had to be able to recognise your driver amongst the throng, remember the type of car and the number plate. So unbeknownst to your wife, partner or mistress, you had to write the number on the back of her neck.

'Darling, what on earth has happened there? You seem to have something on your neck, let me get it off.'

And while you're loudly admiring her sparkling necklace and commenting on her shapely nape, you scribble, somewhat delicately, the necessary information.

The first time we took a limo, we waited for an hour and a half to be picked up and, of course, you would find yourself cheek by jowl with many other attendees. A perfect opportunity to network and to make false promises about how you could help each other further your careers. Much exaggeration and lying about what everyone would do for each other. Every artist or producer I met, while in line, loved my songs and promised a deal. It was all nonsense, as very few of us wielded much power – it was just a game, some kind of Hollywood sporting event with no winners.

I had the good fortune to meet and write a song with the legendary lyricist Don Black. An Oscar winner for 'Born Free', Don was responsible for numerous musicals and a number of huge hits. Over lunch he shared this story with me.

Having come up with an idea for a musical film and being well connected, he made some calls to several big movie studios. One outfit was particularly interested and flew Don over from London to discuss the idea. Five minutes into his pitch, the studio president interrupts, 'Wait a minute, Don. Just hold it there.' He gets on the phone to his PA, 'Shelley, get me head of production, head of advertising, head of promotion, someone from budgeting, press. Bring in the whole team.' He hangs up and continues, 'Don, I want you to pitch to the whole team. They'll love this idea as much as I do.'

Eventually, serious numbers of producers, executives, accountants, flunkies and at least one mogul arrive. They sit enthralled as Don Black delivers a great pitch, complete with demos of the major tunes.

The president is ecstatic. 'Don, you're fantastic. This is fantastic. This is going to be huge. Fantastic! Now where are you staying?'

Don replied, 'the Beverly Wilshire.'

'Of course. Where else is there? That's terrific. We'll be in touch later or at the latest ... first thing tomorrow after we've discussed the budget. Thank you for bringing this to us. We love it and we love you.'

Don drives back to his hotel and rings his wife.

'Darling, the meeting couldn't have gone better. They love my idea. I think we can definitely buy that house in Kensington, put an offer in. The deal should be sorted tomorrow at the latest. Talk to you tomorrow.'

Don never heard from the studio again.

The head of Warner Bros Records in LA, the industry legend Mo Ostin, had to deal with the change of ownership. There was a lot of talk of 'bottom line' and 'quarterly results' and whichever bean counter was in charge, they knew nothing about the business. They didn't like his figures and told him so.

Mo, irritated by this scrutiny, arranged meetings with the entertainment conglomerate DreamWorks, who wanted to set up a music division. At the end of the third quarter when figures were still below management expectations, Warner Bros fired Mo, who happily went to work with Steven Spielberg. At the end of the fourth quarter, when all the albums that Mo had been working on came out, Warners had their best year ever. As we say, in our little band, 'It's people that don't know what they're doing telling the people who do know what they are doing what to do.'

And those are two magnificent examples of what Hollywood can do to even the most successful among us.

When I was working as a record producer, I had a manager and all the attendant necessary bollocks to try and persuade people that I knew what I was talking about. Let's be clear about this, 95 per cent of the people in our industry have little or no clue how to make a hit. Charlie Gillett paraphrased the plight of the artist:

> Members of groups have generally expressed discontent with their relationships with record companies, ranging from being paid low royalties to interference from unsympathetic A&R departments who chose the wrong material, released the wrong singles, failed to promote artists, and any number of other complaints.

A friend of mine once hired Coldplay's producer to work on a record in the expectation that he would bring some of the magic that had made the band such a huge success. Disappointingly, it seemed clear to me that this gentleman had, like the rest of us, just been fortunate enough to be standing in the room when some really talented people went to work.

I've had my fair share of battles with record companies over the years. I produced some tracks for a Rita Coolidge album called *Cherokee* – in tribute to her ancestry. She hadn't recorded for several years and this was a sort of a comeback. She was lovely to work with, very beautiful and spiritual, a real artist, and we recorded some great tracks and wrote one song together, 'Love Lessons'. There was no money up front and even after the recording was completed, the label wouldn't pay me or the musicians involved. I asked the recording studio not to release the finished master tapes to Caliber until they coughed up the dosh. The studio was great and agreed to my 'suggestion'. There were some – let's call them – 'discussions', but the studio stood firm until we got paid.

One record that I worked on disappeared without trace – the result of an ego battle between Disney and CBS over promoting the project. In the end, nobody promoted it, although there was a 35-minute direct-to-video release of music videos using famous Disney sequences and new animation. The idea was the brainwave of B.A. (Brian) Robertson, Glaswegian songwriter, musician and some-time actor. The Disney Corporation had taken up his idea for various modern artists such as Billy Joel, Michael Bolton, Harry Connick Jr and Bobby McFerrin, among others, to record Disney classics. The album was to be called, *Simply Mad About the Mouse: A Musical Celebration of Imagination*. Brian wanted the Gipsy Kings to record a version of the 1940 *Pinocchio* classic, 'I've Got No Strings', and he asked if I would do a demo to give to the band as an example of what it might sound like.

This was going to be a bit of a challenge – although I did own a Spanish guitar, I'm not a flamenco player! To my immense surprise the Gipsy Kings agreed to the proposition and Brian and I flew to Paris to record them. Because I speak a bit of French I was put in charge of the production. I had a very simple strategy; I asked them what their producer would do if he was making this record and they explained the way they worked. Incisively, I announced, 'I think we'll do that then.' I was cooking with gas that day.

The Gipsy Kings were a jolly lot. At one point one of them came in dressed as a woman, having found some ladies' clothes in the dressing room. He wasn't terribly convincing because he sported a beard and possessed an Adam's apple the size of a golf ball. He swept around the room and then exited stage left to a round of applause.

'What should we do next?' I asked, ever the man in charge and still on top form.

The response, 'We've done all the guitars, so let's put on the percussion,' seemed right and proper.

Another band member added, 'We have a show tonight in Belgium, so we'll be on our way.'

Their work completed, the guys left, and the engineer stated that he needed to clear some tracks to put down the percussion and so started to erase some of the unused vocal takes. He was halfway through this process when I noticed the red light was on track eighteen where we had recorded the guitar solos. A four-letter word escaped my lips, 'Heck!' And then, 'Can we get them back?' I was referring to the band not the music, which was lost forever. Somehow, a very useful person got hold of another very useful person, who got hold of the Gipsy Kings before they left for the gig and brought back Tonino Baliardo, the soloist. He played everything again in six minutes and in surprisingly good humour. I wasn't in such good humour with the engineer.

Afterwards, Brian and I found ourselves at Chez Castel, the famous bar in Saint-Germain-des-Prés, where I had hung out with the Ingoes in 1969. Tentatively I knocked on the door, a peephole opened, through which some wrinkled eyes stared at me.

'Hi,' I said tentatively. 'You probably don't remember me. I was in the Ingoes and used to …' Before I could continue, the door opened and there was Le Patron.

'Ah Jim, how nice to see you. Come in. Tell me everything. Tonight, you are my guests. You and your friend will drink for free.'

B.A. was distinctly impressed. 'I should hang out with you more often.'

I was employed as a staff writer at MCA (Music Corporation of America) on a six-figure annual income every year for three years during the 1990s. MCA was a label maintained by MCA Music Entertainment Group, which also owned Universal Pictures and was established in 1972. A pretty powerful outfit. The label's earliest album releases were Elton's *Yellow Brick Road* and the Who's *Quadrophenia*. Not a bad start. MCA was later referred to as 'Music Cemetery of America' by disgruntled musicians and producers.

My publisher Betsy Anthony at MCA was a wonderful woman who looked after me and would send me off around the country to co-write with fellow songwriters. So I'd find myself in Nashville for a week collaborating with people I didn't know. I'd meet the writers for the first time in a designated room on 'Music Row' and had to bare my soul to complete strangers. We'd write for two different sessions a day and were expected to produce ten new songs a week.

Unsurprisingly, none of the songs made it. Starting from scratch it's unlikely that you can get the whole song completed in half a day and so you need time to work on it in your own time. In fact, the best idea came one morning after we'd finished, and one of the writers and I were saying goodbye in the parking lot and talking about our children. I got my guitar out and we wrote the basis of a pretty good song on the back steps of the building. Unfortunately, the cassette is lost, but I thought it was the only one worth finishing.

In 1997, Betsy set me up with Russ Kunkel, celebrated session drummer and member of the Section, the go-to band for singer songwriters, including James Taylor. Russ and I got on like a house

on fire. He's written a lot of great music and is very kind and generous. We wrote for a couple of hours the first afternoon and sorted
out the melody and chords and, based on my love of not working too
hard, we relaxed over a glass or two of wine and planned to meet the
next day to write the lyric. We went to a French bistro on Ventura
Boulevard and were surprised to see Marlon Brando at the back. We
waved, chatted about this and that, he asked us what our hopes and
fears were for the future and if we were really happy. Then we argued
about *Last Tango* and its erotic preoccupations. He next threw a bottle
of Chateau Lafite at us. It was vintage 1999, which surprised us as
this was still 1997. Well, of course, I exaggerate … but he was there
… honestly.

Russ and I chatted – I find that lyrics often come out of conversations. We discussed an article in *Rolling Stone* magazine, which
stated that every generation has its own groove – whether it be
swing, rock, reggae, hip hop, etc. So, we came up with the idea of a
child asking their parents about their taste in music. We also talked
about a foreign language title. A French title maybe? We were in a
French restaurant, after all. I suppose it's a good job we weren't in
Chicago's infamous eatery, 'Ron of Japan'. Anyway, we sat there all
afternoon working on the song that became 'N'Oubliez Jamais'
(Never Forget).

I have to say most of the lyric was written by Russ and when we
had finished, my immediate reaction was that I didn't like that each
line in the chorus rhymed. But I bit my tongue and thought I should
at least give it some time. As I sang it to myself, I realised it did actually work really well – so glad, in retrospect that I didn't mention it to
Russ. Who knows what we might have ended up with …

Sherry Orson was the song plugger at Universal. She was a tough
woman – highly opinionated and very direct. She wanted me to run
my songs past her before I made the studio demos – something I
invariably didn't do! But she did love this song and, entirely through
her efforts, got Joe Cocker to record it for his album *Across from*

Midnight. The song was a number one hit in Europe and played a lot in France for obvious reasons.

I hadn't seen Joe since he came to the studio when we were making *Footloose and Fancy Free* and in those days, he was often quite thirsty. He staggered about in the control room for a while before falling into the multi-track tape machine while it was running. Fortunately, the tape survived. But it was a close call.

Much later when I was touring with Katie Melua, we played a festival in Switzerland with Joe. We spent a very happy hour together in his dressing room and then Katie and I watched him perform. He was in great voice and going down very well with the crowd. Then ... the intro of 'N'Oubliez Jamais' began, the audience recognised the song, rose to their feet and applauded. I was choked up as I had never heard him sing it live. Katie, sensing how emotional and proud I was, gripped my arm in support. It was a wonderful moment for me. A memory I'll always cherish.

Joe had kicked his addiction to drugs and drinks some years before but succumbed to lung cancer in 2014 – the forty cigarettes a day habit had done the damage. He was one of our greatest rock singers and a lovely man, admired and liked in equal measures.

Another lovely guy, John Alexander, was the head of creative at MCA and had a great ear for talent. He had signed Alanis Morrisette to her first publishing and label deals when she was a teenager and worked with her for a couple of years without success. John wanted MCA records to produce her first album, but they just didn't want to know. John had huge faith in Alanis's talent and so went to Maverick, Madonna's label, who later released her first album, *Jagged Little Pill*. The album was expected to sell 250,000 'units' but ended up selling 30 million copies and became *Billboard* magazine's 'Album of the Decade'. John had previously suggested I write with Alanis, and meet up for a drink, which we did. We got on well and talked about our work and the possibility of collaborating. Unfortunately, I was very busy working on other projects at that stage and had to tell John that

I couldn't do anything for a month. In the meantime, she met with Glen Ballard, who is a much better writer than me anyway. Not the best decision I have ever made.

Everyone thought very highly of John Alexander and believed that he should be put in overall control of the publishing division as he had made tens of millions of dollars for them, but no – they pushed him aside and brought in another executive, David Renzer, who fired John two months later. No good deed goes unpunished. John later joined ASCAP (the American Society of Composers, Authors, and Publishers) as a senior executive.

David Renzer also decided that MCA no longer needed Russ and me in the company and let us go. About a year after 'N'Oubliez Jamais' had been released, and had achieved much success, the money started to pour in for MCA. Betsy rang and informed me that she was in the quarterly meeting with the publishing section and David Renzer was going through the sales figures with her. Our song was at number sixteen in the bestselling MCA songs. She reported that the conversation went something like this:

Renzer inquired, 'What's this foreign title?'

Betsy replied, 'It's French.'

'Oh OK. Joe Cocker is terrific. Who the hell are the writers?'

'Russ Kunkel and Jim Cregan.'

'These guys are good.'

Betsy smiled, 'Yes, they are.'

'I never heard of them. What's their status?'

'You fired them last month.'

Betsy couldn't wait to get on the phone to tell me.

During 1997, I started work as a staff producer with Windham Hill records. It was an interesting label and had been formed twenty years previously by hippy college dropout and Bay Area guitarist Will Ackerman and his then girlfriend, Anne Robinson. The releases were mostly instrumental in the early days, a new age eclectic mix of jazz, folk and classical but all (to use the Californian vernacular) could be described as 'mellow'. The label was sold to BMG (Bertelsmann Music Group) – or Big Mean Germans to yet more disgruntled artists – for millions of dollars. Will Ackerman insisted, in the sale, that he was re-signed to the label for a huge fee and a royalty rate that was unheard of. Will had negotiated one of the best agreements in recording history!

I had been lucky ... again. The job at Windham Hill had come about when I wrote a song that Larry Hamby, then head of A&R (Artists and Repertoire) at A&M records liked, a song called 'Love Spoken here', which I'd also co-written with Russ Kunkel and had been recorded by the Neville Brothers. Larry and I got on very well and we kept in touch when he moved to Windham Hill.

As most writers do, when a contact moves to a new organisation, I tried to flog him some dodgy old songs I had lying around. His sidekick over there was Patrick Clifford and the two of them were a great double act. Much fun to be with and one time I went to New York with them just to hang out and look at bands that they were interested in. You had to love them because they maintained a high level of professional optimism in the face of daily disappointment.

BMG acquired another label and dumped it on Larry and Patrick. They were already swamped with work, so Larry called me up and told me that they were now responsible for making twenty records that month. They had no idea how they were going to do it.

'Come and help us out.'

So, they gave me a parking space, a desk and a computer. Funnily enough, despite evidence to the contrary, it didn't feel that I was working for a corporation. I was essentially an independent contractor. I was freelance and not on the official payroll and so didn't have to clock in or out – an arrangement that, as you can imagine, would not have suited me. The whole atmosphere on the floor where I was based was easy going and highly creative. We were just left to get on with it.

I also had access to the fabulous Lori Tedds. Her job title was secretary, but she was invaluable to BMG – the whole organisation would have ground to a halt without her involvement. She was someone that everyone went to for help and advice.

I worked with Janis Ian on a track from her 1999 album, *God and the FBI*. The song was called 'Memphis' and featured such notables as Willie Weeks, Steve Gadd and Chet Atkins. Janis also wanted to sing a duet with Willie Nelson and so she and I flew down to Willie's Texas studio, based in the Pedernales Country Club, near Austin, to record his vocals live.

I have to say, I'm not someone who is star-struck – I've been lucky to meet and know some big names in the entertainment industry and don't go weak at the knees. It's the musician's or actor's work that I admire. It's what they do, not who they are, that impresses me. But when Willie Nelson walked in the room, his presence was incredible. He was extraordinarily charismatic and at 5ft nothing, he stood head and shoulders above numerous celebrities that I had met through the years.

Willie was warm and friendly, and we sat around for a while shooting the breeze. There was a sign outside the studio which read, 'We smoke here' and so, inevitably, he lit up a joint and passed it around. I had stopped smoking dope years before and for a moment I thought I might 'just say no', but I couldn't resist. It was an offer I simply couldn't refuse. And so, I 'just said yes'. I was meant to be in charge but having been heavily stoned from previous experiences on grass, I knew that my critical faculties can disappear and my ability to tell what's right is hampered. When you're stoned, everything sounds good.

Fortunately, Willie made everything effortless. He sang the song two or three times and did a fantastic job. Back in LA, I added Janis' vocals and it sounded terrific. Still does.

Janis is a huge talent and excellent musician on both piano and guitar – she possesses a pure, clear voice, and is an elegant writer of beautifully observed songs. She's not that easy to work with as collaborating doesn't come that naturally to her, but she did pay me one of the nicest compliments I've ever had. As the producer it was my job to see the songs were in the best possible shape before we started recording. So, the unenviable task of making improvements and suggestions fell to me. It's not easy to tell artists that their song isn't quite right and when I offered my two cents' worth to Janis, she was initially somewhat uncomfortable, but did then take my suggestions on board. She later commented, 'You're the best song doctor I have ever worked with.'

Windham Hill released a Christmas album every year and Larry asked me to produce that year's Yuletide treat. He gave me a very generous budget and royalty rate, wished me some early season's greetings and told me to come back when it was completed. This was how I met William Garrett Walden, known as 'Snuffy' to his mates. He is a hugely successful and highly respected television theme composer, and the winner of multiple awards including an Emmy for *West Wing*.

I knew Snuffy Walden's music from Stevie Wonder and Chaka Khan. I really wanted to meet him, and I wasn't disappointed. We got on well and when he was offered his first solo deal, he very generously asked me to produce the album. He really didn't need to – he was a much better producer, writer, programmer and guitar player than me, but needed someone to say, 'That's great, let's keep it.' A role I could easily fulfil. I think my enthusiasm was useful in making decisions.

Snuffy is a rare man. He pulled himself out of a drug and alcohol habit that almost killed him, to become America's foremost composer. He is now married, a father of two and a sponsor of many alcoholics whom he mentors with great compassion. He also plays guitar with blinding clarity. He is so soulful it's a beautiful thing to hear. He has become a lifelong friend and I am privileged to know him.

So, as soon as I finished one album for Larry and Patrick, they would give me another one to produce. It was great work – they just let me get on with it. The Nature Conservancy, an environmental charitable outfit, wanted to put out a record to promote their causes and raise funds. The organisation was based in Arlington, Virginia and I was dealing with these high-powered people in Washington DC. The president of the Nature Conservancy in response to my question, 'How are you saving the wilderness?' replied, 'We do it the American way. We buy it.'

This album allowed me to record one of the songs I had written with Robin Le Mesurier and Bernie Taupin, called 'Stars and Seeds', which seemed a very appropriate number for this lot. The song's lyric suggested a star falling to earth from which a tree grows ... and then a man can climb this tree to heaven. I set about gathering guest singers for this track. There was a huge budget of $35,000, which was the most expensive single I ever made. So, I got my phone book out and asked some of my favourites to sing a verse each. Mavis Staples, Etta James, Righteous Brother Bill Medley, and Peabo Bryson. The rest of the album consisted of licensed tracks and new pieces from artists such as James Taylor and Little Feat. I would describe 'Stars and Seeds' as having escaped rather than being released and the album never came out, as a result of BMG selling Windham Hill. Another victim of record company incompetence.

I was delighted that Rod and I remained friends after I quit the band. We still saw each other socially and I would send him the odd song. Towards the end of 1992 I knew that he was planning an 'unplugged' album and then tour with some of 'the old school', including Ronnie Wood and Kevin Savigar. I was the acoustic guitar player in the original band, took solos and presumed that they would want me on board. The trouble was that no one had called me, and MCA were about to send me on a writing trip to New York at the same time as the recording was due to take place. I called Malcolm Cullimore and said, 'If you're thinking of calling me to do the unplugged record and that I'm sitting around waiting for the call, I'm off to New York ...'

I didn't have to wait long and was delighted to be involved. Sometimes, you need to be proactive! In January 1993, we met up at an LA studio for several weeks of rehearsals. The scene was set by Ronnie arriving in a four-by-four, opening the boot to reveal a selection of wine, beer, a spirit or two, coolers, ice and cocktail paraphernalia, should the mood take us. I've seen worse stocked pubs.

It was great to see 'Woody' again. He's a great guy – I'd known him for years – he was always so friendly and approachable. One bloke who Ronnie could have done without meeting was the legendary record producer Phil Spector. We had been to Robin Le Mesurier's birthday bash and then went on to a party at A&M studios to hear Ronnie's album *Slide on This*. A great gathering with lots of mates, a full bar (even more drinks than sourced from Ronnie's four-by-four) and lots of food.

Phil Spector has done some great things in music but on this evening, he showed a side of him that erased all those good memories. He pulled a gun on Robin Le Mesurier. Here's Robin's account:

> At about three or so in the morning I decided it was time for me to leave. I was looking everywhere to say goodnight to Ronnie and Mac. I couldn't find them anywhere until I was told they were in a little makeshift room within the studio. As I opened the door and entered the room Spector was standing by the wall to my right. He immediately reached into the inside of his jacket, pulled out a gun and pointed the snub-nosed revolver directly in my face. I didn't scream or duck, I just stood there motionless. I was glued to the floor and more than a little freaked out.

Now, Robin is one of the world's finest gentlemen; kind, warm and sensitive and though I didn't see the actual incident, I was right there when, ashen-faced, he came towards me. Fortunately, Ronnie Wood yelled at Spector to put the gun away and no physical harm was done. Spector is now serving time for the murder of Lana Clarkson, a hostess at the House of Blues, a music venue on Sunset Boulevard. So Robin's encounter could have been fatal.

We recorded the live 'unplugged' show on 5 February at Universal Music Studios. It was a pretty intimate atmosphere and it was a special evening. Rod wrote, 'the show seemed to gather a real momentum, and I found myself right back in these songs and connecting emotionally with them a depth I hadn't experienced for years.' The album title, *Unplugged ... and Seated* came from the singer, describing how hard it was to perform while sitting down during the recording of 'Stay with Me'. Songs included 'Every Picture', 'Maggie May', 'Mandolin Wind' and the whole album was something I'm very proud of. It went platinum three times in the USA and Canada and a version of Van Morrison's 'Have I Told You Lately' was released as a single and reached number one in the UK charts. Strangely this song was only added at the last minute and with only a brief run-through before the show, I had no idea that I was going to play a guitar solo but as usual my best work is when I don't think too much.

Jane and Camille would join me whenever possible on the tour. Fortunately we travelled in style, renting the Los Angeles Lakers' basketball team's private jet (I've never had so much leg room!). This meant that we could stay in one place for a couple of weeks, before moving on to the next city and, believe me, when you're away for ten months, that's a bonus.

Halfway into the tour, we played in Florida and were staying at the Ritz Carlton in Palm Beach. It was a particularly happy time. Many of the band had brought their wives and kids, the hotel was right on the beach and apart from the occasional inconvenience of having to go to work, it was a free holiday.

When it was time to leave, Jane started packing and 3-year-old Camille was nowhere to be found. There was no panic, as we knew she was somewhere in the suite and, eventually after an extensive search, we found her curled up inside a large suitcase.

'Hi Darling, there you are! What's going on?'

'Well, Mummy, I thought that if you couldn't pack all your pretty dresses, we wouldn't be able to leave.' She smiled sweetly. Even then she knew her mother really well.

I had one more run-in with Rod's management team after being re-united with him and the band. I found the assistant manager to be self-serving and egotistic. She had a very high opinion of herself. I suppose someone had to. We were playing in LA and she informed the band members that we couldn't have any complimentary tickets. This was unheard of – we always received a couple of tickets each. When we asked why, she replied, 'There are too many VIPs coming to the show to hand out tickets to friends and family.' There was, apparently, nothing she could do about it and in any case, 'It's Rod's idea.'

At that time, I wasn't spending a lot of time with Rod and didn't query it with him. Rod was then married to Rachel Hunter and she bumped into Kim, the wife of keyboard player Ian McLagan. They had a chat and on parting, Rachel said, 'See you at the gig!' Kim replied that she wasn't going because the concert was sold out. 'The band weren't given any tickets. Apparently, Rod knows all about it and is OK with it.'

Rachel accosted Rod later and told him that she thought this was very mean to the band. In fact, Rod didn't know anything about it. It transpired this was a scheme of the assistant manager's and she must have used the tickets for her mates or sold them. She was not my favourite person – it was nothing personal, I just couldn't trust her.

9

Do You Think I'm Sixty?

Marriage is a lot like the army, everyone complains, but you'd be surprised at the large number that re-enlist.

James Garner

Somehow, I had managed to get a meeting with Dolly Parton with a view to producing her next album. There is something quite wonderful about Dolly Parton. Not only is she extraordinary to look at, but she is a gifted songwriter, with a tremendous voice and she can also act. I am given her number and am quite excited to speak to her in person. I suggest meeting at her hotel, but she insists on coming to my house. This is pretty smart on her part as she gets to see how I live, how flash my home is and what kind of motor I'm driving.

So, Dolly finds her way through the maze of tiny streets that eventually brings her to my door. She leaves her handsome driver in the car and comes in. She is quite petite and incredibly charming. Dressed in a low-cut top and a pair of skin-tight trousers, she exudes charisma, laced with huge sex appeal. So how the hell am I going to keep to my plan not stare at her chest?

Endeavouring to impress her with my supreme professionalism, I keep my eyes firmly above her neck. That's not to say I didn't glance at them surreptitiously when I thought she wasn't looking. They are so cartoonlike in proportion to the rest of her that even Jessica Rabbit would be envious. But I wanted her to know that those bosoms were not influencing me in any way.

The relationship between artist and producer is quite complex – the producer's job is to help the artist make the very best record at that moment in their career. So, you are part psychologist, cheer-leader, musical guru, whipping boy, confessor and guv'nor. You're permanently caught in that no man's land between the record com-pany, the artist, their management and the musicians. You can never wear too many hats. Crash helmets included. And with Dolly there are these extra couple of things to consider.

Dolly and I have tea. I might as well make the most of any per-ceived Britishness. Occasionally, being from Britain has its advantages in the USA. We talked about music and songwriting and performing and generally all the stuff we had in common. She was an absolute delight; beautifully mannered, with a soft drawl, she was the epitome of a southern belle.

In conversation, I had mentioned it was Jane's birthday the next day. Jane called out from another room that she needed to take my car to do some shopping as hers was being serviced.

'OK,' I shouted back. 'I just need to get something from it before you go.'

'Her birthday presents are in the car,' I whispered to Dolly. 'I need to get them out and put them in the studio. I won't be a minute.' I slipped out to the driveway and while I was gone, Jane stepped into the living room as she hadn't heard my exit line.

'Where's he gone?' she asked Dolly.

'To his car.'

'Really? Why?'

'He's gone down to the car to get your fuckin' presents 'cause that's where the motherfucker's bin hidin' 'em,' Dolly replied with a shit-kicking grin. 'He's gonna stash your shit in the studio.' Even Jane, who is not easily shocked, was a little taken aback by Dolly's ... shall we say 'directness'. But, you know, girls together. I returned in complete ignorance of what had just gone down and continued to behave with my best impersonation of the British gentleman. And Dolly resumed her perfect poise.

I didn't get the job – perhaps had I behaved in a less polite way and had made it clear quite how impressed I was with her statuesque appearance, things might have, in my mind, been different. Maybe. Dolly did after all once say, 'It costs a lot of money to look this cheap!' She either found a better producer or I had played it all wrong. It was, in any case, a treat to meet such an iconic figure and have so much fun with her.

I didn't have the same problem with Bernie Taupin. Not that he didn't have a magnificent chest, but I just wasn't drawn to his pectorals in the same way. In this instance, there was no dichotomy, and so, in 1996, I was invited to join him in starting a new band, Farm Dogs. I had known Bernie since I had been on Elton's tour, back in the 1970s. Apart from being a superb, imaginative lyricist, he was also a pretty good vocalist. My old mucker Robin Le Mesurier was also on board and had recommended me to Bernie. The band was completed by the addition of Dennis Tufano, a singer with the Buckinghams in the 1970s. Bernie had also recruited David Cole, a recording engineer and co-producer for the project.

Bernie wanted to work at his beautiful horse ranch in Santa Ynez, about a two-hour drive north of Los Angeles, near Santa Barbara. The racquetball court had been turned into a studio, and we wrote, rehearsed and recorded in this idyllic setting. Because Bernie had already stockpiled a huge number of lyrics, we were able to complete up to two songs a day. At our most prolific, on one day, we produced two and a half songs between 10 a.m. and 6 p.m. We worked out the song format, depending on the lyric, using only acoustic guitars.

Apart from the work, which was hugely enjoyable, the daily routine was as much fun. After breakfast, we would head into Santa Ynez to buy food and drink provisions for dinner that night. Every morning, at the El Rancho supermarket, the proprietor would suggest a wine for the evening and then ask for Bernie's opinion. Bernie would sniff the wine, roll it around in the glass, take another sniff, take a sip, swill it around in his mouth, swallow hard and then invariably reply, 'Might do for a breakfast wine.' As soon as the working day was over, it was time for the imbibing of a very large Martini. And to paraphrase Hawkeye Pierce in *Mash*, 'It had to be dry enough to still have dust on the olive.' We would all then set to work in the kitchen preparing dinner from all the local produce and eventually sit down to a riotous meal. Sometimes with wine.

It's funny how many musicians I know that are pretty good cooks. This certainly applied to Farm Dogs; although I was only ever the sous-chef, fit only for peeling potatoes and opening bottles, I learned a lot from these guys. Bernie and his wife Stephanie opened a hugely successful restaurant in LA called Cicada which was the setting for the Farm Dogs' first ever gig. Robin, at one time, was approached to start a TV show about cooking entitled *Rock 'N' Roll Cuisine*. Unfortunately, it never happened although his first wife published a book with the same title.

The first album *Last Stand in Open Country* was released in 1996 and two of our songs, 'This Face' and 'Last Stand in Open Country', were covered by Willie Nelson on his album *The Great Divide*, which was nominated for best country album. Although we hardly sold any CDs the few that did escape ended up with some influential people who suggested the songs to Willie. Thanks guys.

There were a couple of changes in personnel for the second album *Immigrant Sons*. Dennis Tufano left, Tony Brock sat in on drums, and Billy Payne, Little Feat's keyboard player, was recruited. He was ridiculously good. Billy could produce brilliant solos after hearing the music for the first time and could listen to every chord change just once and be able to repeat it flawlessly. Tad Wadhams joined the band playing bass and recalled:

> I'll never forget Robin and Jim Cregan teaching me how to play an old school 1950s-style rock groove! I was a bit indignant at first when they told me gently that I was playing the bass groove WRONG, since, after all, I was the American in the band! They patiently dissected the beat, told me exactly what to play. Tony Brock entered with the proper drum beat (which of course he already knew how to play), Robin and Jim kicked in with the guitar figures and the whole rehearsal studio lifted into the air and flew away!

A US tour was planned to promote the album for which Bernie most generously put in $100,000. This was supposed to be equally matched by our record company headed by Seymour Stein. He failed to live up to the agreement. No surprises there. Their promises were broken pretty well all through the tour. No publicity or support worth a damn.

We were reunited with our old friend Pete Buckland as tour manager and we had a great time. Bernie insisted we should take care of our culinary needs by using the *Zagat* guide to the finest restaurants in each city. Heaven knows how much he spent but it was an education I was happy to receive. Although we didn't play huge venues, we did go to the major cities and played their established rock clubs like the Bottom Line in New York. We performed at the Roxy on Sunset Boulevard, which was a sell out and a great show. Hometown boys make good.

Unfortunately, Bernie's marriage to Stephanie was in trouble and, on our return, he needed time to reflect and heal. He did this partially by throwing himself into fine art. Large canvasses were produced in multimedia and extraordinary abstract works were created resulting eventually in his own exhibition.

Sadly, the band didn't play again. We all went our separate ways but what a great time we had.

In 1999, Robin and his girlfriend, Jules, were married at the ranch by Tad, who held a licence from some dubious ministry. There were about eighty guests, a Mariachi band and much tequila. Farm Dogs performed, Kiefer Sutherland sang 'Knockin' on Heaven's Door' and Rod sang 'Sweet little Rock and Roller'.

I was best man and this, for those of you who weren't there, is my wedding toast:

This will be a toast made by an Irishman to a French-sounding Englishman who's marrying an Italian-American at a Californian ranch hosted by an English cowboy-lyricist and performed by a monopedic musician-minister who is not even from here … but who is? This is a great occasion for making friends, getting re-acquainted with some old ones, settling scores, and burying hatchets. Drinking, dancing, and celebrating the blessing of love. Love, without which we would not have reason to gather today.

For not only is it the force of life itself, it is also so singularly the most popular topic for songwriters and … 'Ain't Love Been Good to Me?' Robin and I have been friends for twenty years or so and we are still waiting to have a row … give it time. There is obviously no rush!

And I am so honoured to be best man today. We have toured the world together in pursuit of the perfect Martini and some of them have occasionally come close. Still the search goes on. He is the kindest of men, his generosity of spirit is boundless, and his quiet depth of understanding is remarkable in one so young. And this love affair with Julie is just the beginning of the really good stuff. Julie said one day that this is a hard crowd to get to know, and she is right. We protect each other as any family does. We support one another, and as she has become beloved of us all, she is seeing that strength surrounding and nurturing her. We cannot choose our blood family but when your friends become family to you, you have the best of it all.

I propose this toast to Robin and Julie; may their love endure all seasons and inspire the sacred in us all.

While one marriage was just starting, another was breaking up – mine.

My son Mackenzie, 'Mack' was born on 9 August 1996, coinciding with our wedding anniversary. Jane's waters broke in the middle of our celebratory dinner at the Peninsula Hotel in Los Angeles and the evening ended at Cedars-Sinai with Jane giving birth via a planned Caesarean. Mack's birth was, however, less dramatic than Camille's arrival.

Soon after, Ruth Kennedy, Jane's mum, moved in with us. She wasn't infirm, but was living alone in Palm Desert, near Palm Springs in the Coachella Valley, and wanted to be near her daughter and grandchildren. I was fine with this. I liked Ruth and recalled Robert, my brother-in-law's, generosity in taking in my dad when he needed looking after in those years before. I wanted to reciprocate by taking in Jane's mother. It was the right thing to do.

Ruth was mainly fine – although she was definitely old school and part of the Daughters of the American Revolution (DAR), an organisation formed of women who can prove lineal blood-line descent from an ancestor who fought in the American War of Independence. Since its original formation, I'm pleased to say that membership is now open to all women, regardless of race or religion. In fact, Camille has now been inducted into the DAR. The initiation took place at our home in Hancock Park amid much pomp and ceremony. I could see the strain in Camille's eyes from trying to keep it together during the formalities, but we all agreed Ruth would have been very proud.

Jane's stepfather was George Kennedy, a professor at UCLA. Together, the Kennedys possessed an extensive art collection and one of the largest private orchid collections in the world. Ruth was an intrepid traveller and on one of her many orchid collecting trips through the Andes, she rode with a broken leg on the back of a donkey, and then, on crutches, made her way through the wild to find new species. Ruth was highly educated, doughty, and I have to say, pretty cool, but she was used to getting her own way. There was some friction at times – she would throw a hissy fit occasionally about the untidiness of the house and insisted on ringing a handbell to summon the housekeeper at dinner time!

Ruth and I got on quite well, but Jane found living with her mother difficult. Ruth's behaviour affected Jane, who became more grumpy and felt frustrated and harried by her mother's presence. Within a couple of years of Mack's birth, our marriage was beginning to fall apart for various reasons. Not all to do with the presence of Jane's mother.

I'm glad to report things are now comfortably civil between us but it took a long while for me to move on from the unpleasantness of the divorce. At the time, I thought my only choices were to evict the wife and mother-in-law or leave myself. So ... I moved in with Robin and Jules and I was very grateful to them for taking me in when I needed help. I was angry and upset and needed the support of my friends. The separation soon proved acrimonious and to quote my friend Steve Moose, 'You get all the justice you can afford.'

Thankfully, I managed to see the kids a lot as Robin and Jules' house was within walking distance of the family home, but there was no spare bedroom for them to stay. Jane and I tried to make the arrangement as easy as possible for the kids, but, being older, Camille found the new living situation difficult. Particularly when Kathleen Keane entered my life.

In 2000, I produced *Tree*, a record for Gaelic Storm, a very talented Irish American folk/rock band, who had begun performing in a Santa Monica pub, but had achieved some success and notoriety by being the steerage party band featured in the film *Titanic*. Kathleen, who hailed from Chicago, was a violinist and composed some of the group's material. In her youth, she had been described as 'a child prodigy on the tin whistle' – and not just by her. *Tree* got to number two on the Billboard World Music chart. We co-wrote a song, 'The Longing', which appeared on Windham Hill's *Celtic Christmas Silver Anniversary* album and topped the same chart for a month.

Apart from being very talented and a lovely person, Kathleen was also beautiful with thick dark wavy hair and devilish blue eyes, filled with mischief. I was smitten and, luckily, so was she. She moved in to Robin and Jules' house with me and we were very happy, although it was very hard for Camille to accept that I was in a relationship and living with a woman who wasn't her mother. There were some difficult times.

Rod was now living with Penny Lancaster, a photographer, model and subsequently a television personality and columnist. They are still together, and she is absolutely delightful and has made Rod the happiest I've ever seen him. They have a wonderful relationship – not to mention two sons, Alastair and Aiden. At that time, Kathleen and I were invited on several holidays with the two of them at Rod's house in Palm Beach and while there, were often guests at various dinners and functions by local socialites.

Bill Koch is one of the four multi-millionaire Koch brothers – Charles and David being the infamous members of the dynasty, who are committed to funding conservative causes and right-wing think tanks. In fact, Bill and brother Frederick have fought a number of legal battles over two decades with their siblings.

Bill Koch, himself, has a bob or two stashed. According to Forbes, in 2018 he was worth about $1.72 billion, thanks to oil and other investments. His yacht, *America 3*, was the winner of the America's Cup in 1992, which was of great interest to me. He was also a well-known art collector. Anyway, Bill and his then fiancée, now wife, Bridget Rooney (granddaughter of the original owner of the Pittsburgh Steelers football team) invited Rod and all his guests to dinner. Apart from Rod and Penny, Robin and Jules, Kathleen and me, there was also Alan 'Big Al' Sewell and his wife Debbie, a former Olympic diver. Big Al is a used car and scrap dealer from Ilford, who is a larger-than-life character in every way. Not only is he built like a brick outhouse, he is hugely entertaining and straight talking. Both he and Debbie possess hearts of gold and are game for all sorts of mischief.

Bill Koch's house was an ocean-front, numerous-roomed, mega-mansion with two swimming pools. Before dinner, our charming host decided to show us around his $15 million wine cellar and asked if any of us had any particular vintage we would like to see. Robin immediately piped up, 'Any Pétrus?'

'Oh yes,' answered Bill, 'I have some.' Pétrus was then worth about $1,000 a bottle. 'Let me open a case.' He produced a bottle and then after a pause, added, 'Since we've opened the case, why don't we try a few more?'

Out of politeness, we drank eight bottles at dinner.

After we'd dined, a slightly inebriated Mr Koch, who by then had taken a shine to Kathleen as everyone always did, gave us a tour of the ground floor of the house. This took over an hour due to his extraordinary collection of astonishing art pieces and artefacts. There was a Picasso here, a Monet there, and paintings by Matisse and Braque adorned the walls. Walking through his house, it was as if the pages from my favourite art books were coming to life. There was an old Western-themed room filled with the work of the American painter, illustrator and sculptor Frederic Remington, as well as Winchester rifles and Colt 45s, Indian dresses and a selection of ornate spurs. Other 'salons' hosted bronzes, Greek and Roman antiquities and, most interesting to me, an enormous room with 6ft long scale models, in stunning detail, of every yacht that had won the America's Cup. It was an extraordinary evening and an experience not to be forgotten.

The next day, Bridget noticed us having lunch in Palm Beach, and stopped to say hello. We briefly referred to the extraordinary multi-million-dollar treasures and one of the greatest private art collections we had seen the night before, to which Big Al said, in his gruff East End accent, 'Bridget, please thank Bill. It was very nice of him take the time to show us his bits and bobs.'

Oh Al, we do love you ...

Kathleen and I enjoyed being with each other, but the biggest problem was that she was rather too many years younger than me. She wanted to start a family in five years' time. I was daunted by this and felt that I would be too old to start a new family and naturally Kathleen didn't want just one child. We decided to part. In the long term we sadly had to face up to the fact that the timing of this relationship just wasn't right for us.

Several months after the split with Kathleen, I came home for a holiday to see the family and re-group. I stayed with Mike Batt at his home, Ewshot Hall, for a little while. As luck would have it, he was just starting work on Katie Melua's first album and asked me if I wanted to help. I did. Katie was just 19 and new to the business but *Call Off the Search* sold 1.8 million copies and went to number one in the charts. Mike asked me if I wanted to join the upcoming tour. I did. Katie's second album *Piece by Piece* also got to the top of the charts and I ended up touring the world with her for five years.

With a number of other musicians, we were invited to play at Nelson Mandela's Aids charity 46664 in South Africa with a number of other musicians and groups. Katie had been asked to sing with Queen which was a great thrill for her as she'd been a lifelong fan. So my pal Roger Taylor was there and we had a few days to catch up and share some stories.

Just before I left the UK, I had received a 'Flat Stanley' from Mackenzie.

Flat Stanley is a character in a children's book, who starts life as an outline of a boy, which is then coloured in by a child. The kids then send the illustration to a friend nearby or anywhere in the world, often having their photograph with Stanley, before returning the said document. Results are often posted on noticeboards at school where children discuss Stanley's travels and adventures.

It just so happens that the day F.S. arrives from Mack I am seeing Rod and Penny and so I take a photograph of them. The next thing Stanley and I know we are in South Africa, hanging out with Nelson Mandela himself, Queen, Paul Rogers, Annie Lennox, and (most importantly for Mack) actor Will Smith. Incredibly, I managed to get them all to pose with Flat Stanley; Will Smith, who needed no intro-duction or explanation to the concept, immediately exclaimed, 'Flat Stanley! I love him, this is so cool' and grinned widely for the photo. I just wish I could have been in the classroom when Mack made his Flat Stanley presentation.

Katie Melua was lovely, very thoughtful and mature for her age. She didn't want any special treatment. Even if a limo had been pro-vided for her, she gave it to the crew or make-up lady and would always travel with the musicians and would give lifts to anyone who needed a ride – whether they were in the band or not!

Mike treated us with affection and respect. We stayed in the most beautiful hotels and always travelled first class. He is a hugely talented writer, arranger, conductor and Womble. He has what I consider to be a very eccentric way of working. I had worked a lot for Mike as a session guitarist over the years and it was unusual for him to use an untrained musician like me. When I'm with Mike, I'm sometimes the only person in the room who can't read music – I guess he is hoping I might add something spontaneous. He once had a 32-bar orchestral break in one of the songs, which he hadn't yet recorded. He had only a click track but knew it was to be in G minor, so he asked me to improvise an acoustic solo for 32 bars whilst listening to just a click. Cheeky, to say the least. But it turned out OK. Another time he gave me a chord chart – then realised after we had actually started recording that he hadn't written out all the chords and so yelled them in my ear and expected me to play them instantly as we recorded. Somehow, I managed.

Mike often employed guitarist Chris Spedding and sometimes both of us together. I remember Chris looking at a particularly complicated music chart and asking, 'Bar 51, Mike? Is that a chord or a telephone number?'

One day whilst relaxing at Mike's house over breakfast and newspapers, we came across an article about how celebs want to be treated after they'd died. Surprisingly, I read that my friend, singer Paul Young thought that I had died and mentioned he wanted to be given the same send-off as I had supposedly been given. Namely, to have his ashes scattered over the countryside from a helicopter. Checking in the mirror and taking my pulse, I figure there's been a small but important mistake.

'I'd better write to the *Daily Blah* in case some of my friends believe I've gone over,' I muse to Batt who is certainly enjoying the moment. (In any case, little did Paul know that employing this method of scattering ashes is pointless, as they just blow back, covering everyone in the cabin with someone else's remains.)

So, Mike comes up with a very good idea to straighten out the confusion in regard to my demise. Firstly, I get a great pair of angel's wings with real feathers and put them on over a white suit and shirt but no shoes or socks. Batt invites Paul Young over to his London apartment to discuss a fictional project. A photographer, who is in on the joke, is also invited and Mike explains to Paul that the photojournalist is documenting a day in the life of Mike Batt.

So, the scene is set. Mike brings up the subject of my death and accompanied by some church music I make my entrance. Hands folded together in prayer, I slowly walk into the room in a death-like trance. Paul leaps to his feet, pointing at me and making strange noises before he figures it out and calls the three of us every name in the book. We hugged for a bit and he even appeared relatively happy I was still alive. Even so, I threatened to sue him unless he took us out to lunch. The photos appeared in the press the following day, so my resurrection was complete.

I've been friends with Andy Hill for as long as I can remember. He is a prolific songwriter for acts as diverse as Bucks Fizz, Diana Ross, Celine Dion, the Wanted and even Eminem, and he has penned more chart hits as just a writer than anyone else I know. He is also an excellent musician and producer.

In 2002, Andy introduced me to Mandy Perryment, who was a dancer, model and actress. She began her career as a child actor and continued performing in West End musicals and on screen until 1998 when she became a casting director for TV, theatre, film and commercials. I fell for Mandy straight away and although I was still residing in Los Angeles, she invited me to stay with her in her house in Surrey. Once it was clear we were committed to each other, I went back to LA, sold almost everything I had left over from the divorce, which wasn't much, and came home, clutching my clothes, my dozen guitars and my fifty-odd platinum records.

The transition back to my homeland was partially complete, but I didn't have my children, who stayed with their mother in LA. The decision to return to the UK was the right one on some levels, but the thought of being thousands of miles away from Camille and Mackenzie was something that I was terribly worried about. Foolishly I believed we would be able to handle the separation. In fact, I had no idea how much heartache this would cause us. I thought I could go back and forth, and they'd come over regularly and it would all be OK, but no matter how many times I made the trip, I just wasn't around the corner to share their daily lives. We spoke on the telephone as much as possible but my relationship with the kids just wasn't the same for some years.

And for this I am forever regretful.

Just thinking about it still hurts.

One summer, during the early days of my romance with Mandy, Rod and Penny very generously invited us to go on holiday with them to their home in the south of France. This is exactly my kind of holiday. After staying in hotels for most of my touring life, they hold little appeal, even if they are very glamorous and hideously expensive. As a professional insomniac, I like to be able to get up, make myself a sandwich, pad about the living room or put my feet up on the sofa and read a book without disturbing anybody.

Their house is high up in the hills above Nice and you can see down to the Mediterranean or across to St Paul de Vence. It's the perfect holiday house. It's not so big as to need a team of people to look after it but there is plenty of room. It's an upside-down house and, like many of those homes built into the hillside, it appears to be a single-storey from the driveway. Most of the bedrooms are on the ground floor with French windows, opening onto a lawned area. There is the swimming pool to one side of the house and a large paved area with sun loungers and umbrellas. Not too shabby.

One of the interesting things about hanging out with Rod is that he has a large and varied set of acquaintances that live in the vicinity of his various homes. Far from being a recluse he will often have the neighbours round for drinks or go out to dinner with them. On this particular evening, he invited this other couple for a quick cocktail before setting off for dinner. As we were checking that the wine was all right, Rod told me that the gentleman I was about to meet was a very good guy but could not help himself when it came to name-dropping about the rich and famous.

Then, one of us came up with the idea that for every famous name mentioned at dinner we would break off a crumb from our French bread and leave it on the tablecloth. Now you know that when you break crusty French bread with your fingers, bits flake off and go all over the place, so it wasn't going to be too obvious. This added an element of foolishness to the upcoming evening.

The couple arrived, and we stepped on to the terrace off the living room, sipping our drinks and admiring the view. The restaurant we were going to was in a beautiful old medieval building that had once been a monastery. We nipped down the hill in a giant SUV with the girls all diamonds and hairspray and wafted down the path and into the joint. The six of us sat down and ordered drinks and appetisers. We were dining in a delightful courtyard, scented with lavender bushes and lit by candlelight. It reminded me of Yeovil where I was born ... apart from the lavender, candlelight and medieval architecture.

Boom! Moments into the evening our guests mentioned Richard Burton and Elizabeth Taylor. Well that was a big start. Crumbs immediately appeared close to the butter dish. These two famous film stars had stayed with our friends in the very house opposite Rod and Penny's. Next came Anthony Newley and Peter O'Toole. A morsel of baguette appeared near the salt cellar. I countered these A-list names with Cilla Black but failed dismally to impress.

The evening progressed along similar lines until by the end of dessert there was small mountain of bread in the centre of the table.

'What the hell's with you two and the bread?' our distinguished friend inquired.

Arghhh ... I immediately feigned a choking fit to cover up my laughter and Rod, ever the gentlemen, leaped to his feet to escort me to the bathroom with a jolly shout of 'I'll come with you!'

Soon we were safely ensconced in a marble tribute to ancient plumbing.

'We've been tumbled,' he said, grinning widely. 'Even I wasn't expecting that many names.'

'There's enough bread there to feed a Flock of Seagulls.'

'Don't you bloody well start, too.'

'How are you going to get me out of this?'

'What do you mean, me?'

'Well, it was your idea.'

'Bollocks!'

'Well we are going to have to come up with something pretty good.'

'How about it's a kind of edible rosary and every time you say a Hail Mary to yourself you break off a bit of bread?'

'That's never going to work; anyone can see you're a semi-devout heathen. And anyway, isn't it a bit insulting that you are praying under your breath while he's regaling us with stories of the rich and famous?'

'You come up with something then.'

'We were having a bet about how many bits of bread we could put on the table before a waiter came along with one of those weird silver scraper things to clear it up.'

'That's not bad, let's go with that.'

Relief.

All that remained was the bare-faced lying. So, as casually as possible, we returned the table only to find the waiter had cleared everything up.

'Oh no!' we cried in unison. 'Now we'll never know.'

'Know what?' our guest demanded.

'Oh, nothing important, it was just a bet and Jim lost.'

I tried to explain but even mentioning that the idea had come from Alvin Stardust made no impression. You just need to know when you're outclassed.

Mandy and I were living very cosily in Surrey. She had converted the garage into a studio and life was pretty good. There was still the constant ache from missing the children, but there was much more work here than in LA, where I had been struggling.

One day, Mandy woke up and said, 'I think I have to have a baby.'

Wow. This was a big surprise. Up until this very moment, she had maintained that she didn't want children. But she was now 44 and I was 58. I was worried that we might both be too old, but Mandy realised it was now or never for us. I was a little cautious at first, but soon fully embraced the idea and became excited at the thought of being a parent again.

Ava Elodie Cregan was born on 14 September 2005 at Kingston upon Thames hospital. Visiting Mandy the following day, I was making myself a cup of tea when a lady joined me in the kitchen.

'How's your daughter doing?' she asked.

'Very well thank you,' I replied.

'And how's the baby?

At that moment, I knew that this would be the continuing pattern of my future relationship with the general public. But I now take great pleasure in telling them that I am the father and revelling in their embarrassment.

When Ava was 8 weeks old, she developed pyloric stenosis – a blockage at the stomach outlet. She was really quite ill and couldn't keep her food down. Her projectile vomiting was so lethal that we were encouraged to re-decorate her bedroom. We rushed her to hospital to be told by the head of paediatrics that it could not be pyloric stenosis because she was too young, and that Ava was suffering from a stomach bug. I wasn't happy with this diagnosis. Immediately alarm bells rang as I knew in my heart that her illness was much more serious than that.

I asked for a second opinion and eventually they made the correct diagnosis – what I had originally thought, pyloric stenosis. As Mr Anthony Aloysius Hancock once remarked, 'I could have been a doctor, but never really bothered.' Ava would need surgery. I asked the doctor, worrying about a future giant scar across her abdomen, 'Can she have keyhole surgery for this?'

'No, they don't make instruments that small.'

'What a load of bollocks,' I thought.

So, Mandy and I shot back home, logged on to the computer and immediately up popped the possibility of keyhole surgery at Great Ormond Street Children's Hospital.

'Ah ha,' I thought.

In one phone call I arranged for an ambulance to collect Ava that night and whisk her up to London. But nothing is ever quite that easy. Returning to the hospital in Kingston upon Thames, we were told she could not be discharged without permission from the head of department, who had gone home.

While we waited for an answer, we sat in a local restaurant, pushing food around our plates and sipping coffee. My phone rang. It was Rod calling from LA.

'Hey pal, just thinking about you. I'll be back in UK soon and we need to get together and have dinner or something. How's it going?'

'Hi kid, nice to hear from you but things are a bit messed up here at the moment.' I explained the situation.

'Oh no, we can't have any of that. Get Ava to over to Great Ormond Street, and I'll pay for everything. Think of it as an early Christmas present.'

'That's an amazing offer, thanks so much. I'll call the hospital and get back to you.'

When we went back to the administrator, the approval had been given and by about 1 a.m., Ava was in the ambulance. She made a complete recovery and is virtually scar-free. So, in the end we didn't need Rod's help, but it was typical of him to volunteer so generously. What a good guy.

We were a very happy little family, but Mandy knew how much I missed Camille and Mackenzie. On my 60th birthday, she threw a surprise party for me with loads of my friends and family. The greatest surprise, however, was the moment when from behind a counter, up jumped Camille and Mackenzie. We screamed in excitement and hugged each other and I couldn't hold back the tears. This was the best birthday present I had ever received. I had no idea that Mandy had arranged and paid for the kids to come over. She had somehow managed to keep them hidden from me before the party. It was a great feat of organisation and she knew how much this would mean to me.

10

Still Making Waves

We don't stop playing because we grow old; we grow old because we stop playing.

George Bernard Shaw

Unfortunately, it turned out that Mandy and I were not as happy or compatible as we both had expected and after a few years, we sadly decided to separate. There had been no infidelity but rather an increasing distancing of how we both wanted to live. I had that Irish open house approach to our home and Mandy was far more private. I didn't handle any of this very well. I could have behaved differently but it was extremely tough on both of us.

I had had such high hopes for this relationship. I dreamed of us getting married and growing old together. I felt an acute sense of failure as I had committed to leaving LA and starting a new family only to see it all turn to dust. It had hurt Camille and Mackenzie to be separated from me by such a distance and now it was all in pieces. The place was littered with broken hearts.

I retreated to Joyce and Robert's house in Dorset to lick my wounds and figure out what to do with my life. Ava was only

2 or 3 years old and Mandy and I both wanted to be with her so for a while, during the week, she stayed with Mandy in Ripley and I drove up from the coast, collected her for the weekend and returned her to Mandy on the Sunday – a total of 400 miles. Not an ideal situation. I needed to move and be close enough to Ava to see her easily.

I was rescued by my dear friend Sarah Thompson, who had a charming guest house in the grounds of her home in Ockham. Mandy and I had worked out a schedule that worked fairly well and, now that I had a place for Ava to stay, things were definitely improving. We spent one of the funniest summers I can remember in this cottage alongside Sarah with barbeques most nights and the guys in the band singing and playing by candlelight under the stars.

I was warmly welcomed by her friends John and Julia Scott, who were particularly generous, throwing a 65th birthday party for me. All was well until Sarah met a man, it became a bit overcrowded and I needed to move out. As I was walking to the shops in Cobham, I saw this blonde lady driving a remarkable vintage 1930s Bentley convertible. Ingrid Dupre, ex-wife of Chris Tarrant, the original host of TV's *Who Wants to Be a Millionaire*, was leaving the supermarket in this beast of a car. We knew each other from earlier days when we had discussed starting our own radio station …

'Ingrid!' I yelled. 'What a fantastic car.'

She pulled over and grinned.

'It used to be my father's, it's been in the family for ever.'

I told Ingrid that I was looking for a flat or house nearby as Ava was now attending Notre Dame school in Cobham. Ingrid's response was music to my ears.

'That's amazing! I have just finished rebuilding an apartment in my house and you can stay there if you want. I'm just around the corner down a country lane.' She didn't bother mentioning that her house was a ten-bedroom affair with a swimming pool and tennis court on three acres of parkland.

'I'll take it,' says I, feeling luck was on my side that day, knowing that Ingrid would be great fun to hang out with. She also had a heart of Norwegian gold.

And it was so.

We did a fair amount of socialising as Ingrid knew so many people, but she was equally happy going to the local pub on quiz nights or staying up late doing shots of vodka, just to keep in practice. One afternoon when we were supposed to blunder about on the tennis court, she got a call from a guy in the village who restored Aston Martins.

'I've got something of interest,' he says.

'Come on over, let's see what you've got.'

Up the drive came the original Aston Martin DB 5 that was used in the James Bond films *Goldfinger* and *Thunderball*, both of which starred Sean Connery. The real thing!

The guy took us to Wisley, an old disused Second World War airfield just down the road in Ockham and we all took turns in driving it down the runway. A schoolboy's dream – and I suppose for Ingrid, a schoolgirl's dream! The car drove brilliantly but, as our host explained, he had yet to start on the full restoration, and so it was going to get even better. The Aston Martin had all the trick stuff used in the film. The machine guns popped out of the side lights, the number plates flipped round, the bulletproof shield rose up from the back and the radar actually worked! I was still unable to remove the grin from my face as we went to lunch. Cars stopped in the road to watch it go by, their eyes drawn to the JB 007 plate. I discovered later that during the renovations, an offer of £6 million was made before it went to auction. The owner refused. Imagine how grumpy he was when it eventually sold for £2.6 million instead.

I later discovered that Ingrid was also a pretty good mechanic and was absolutely fearless at taking on any adventure, including a fortnight's holiday in Iran!

Another extraordinary woman with whom I had the great good fortune to be friends was Caron Keating, one of the loveliest people in the world and a friend of Robin Le Mesurier. He and his wife Jules were living off the Kings Road in Fulham at the time and when I was visiting from LA, I'd stay with them. Caron often came around for dinner or just to hang and she was an absolute diamond. Funny, beautiful, bright and witty, she was an exceptional girl. We became great mates and when she was in LA she stayed at my house for a week. Caron was a presenter on *Blue Peter*, the kids' TV show that is even older than some of my suits and she, along with co-presenter Yvette Fielding, was in California to film a show about sharks, *Diving with Sharks*.

'Are you sure you want to do this? Doesn't diving with sharks involve ... some ... sharks?' I asked intelligently.

'Of course,' Caron replied firmly.

'You're kidding, right?'

'No, it'll be OK, they've got the guys from the James Bond films as protection in the water with me.'

'You mean the ones that are still alive?' I ventured.

'Anyway, you're coming with me, aren't you?'

'I suppose I am now,' I said, attempting to be gallant and wondering what 'with me' meant ...

Fortunately, when we arrived at the marina mooring of the 60ft sport fisherman yacht, there wasn't a spare wet suit or tanks. Relief flooded through me like a shot of tequila, although publicly, I feigned much disappointment.

Caron emerged from the cabin, ready to go. The shark cage was dangling from a spar leaving it just above the swells and it looked fairly flimsy. The theme from Jaws was running through my head like a shoal of mackerel. The top of the cage flips open and she clambers in. Once secured, it is lowered into the water which had been thoroughly chummed.

'Here they come,' someone yells and sure enough several dorsals break the surface next to the boat.

'They're not that big,' I heard a shark wrangler remark.

Thank God, I thought. What's she going through down there?

I can't really see too much with the movement of the waves and the reflected light, so I lean over the transom to get a better look. Suddenly I am pulled upright roughly by a crew member.

'You don't wanna be doing that,' he whispers, still holding me by the back of my collar. 'They'll take yer face off.'

'Ahh. Thanks for that,' I mutter, feeling like a bloody idiot.

Meanwhile we can make out the underwater cameraman is shooting away outside the cage and a quartet of Bond's old minders with electric shark sticks are saving his limbs from becoming lunch.

'OK, let's get her to leave the cage and swim round to the ladder at the stern,' the director says, with a casual disregard for fishy appetites.

'Are you sure?' I say, eyeing the sharks with some trepidation.

'Yeah she'll be all right,' he says, all nonchalance and bravado.

'Bet you wouldn't do it, you tosser,' I murmur under my breath.

But, bless her, she did, and although she was trembling like a lip about to reveal a secret, she had that gleam in her eye that said it all.

Tragically, Caron was taken from us at the age of 41 from breast cancer. Years later, after I had moved back to the UK, I heard from Caron's mother, Gloria Hunniford, herself a British national treasure. TV presenter, disc jockey, reporter and author, she turned the tragedy and insufferable pain of her daughter's death into a successful and respected charity, the Caron Keating Foundation. I don't know how she does it. So petite, she brings a whirlwind of energy into the room and sweeps everyone along with her. She is smiling and kind, with a moment for everyone. I am genuinely impressed.

In 2015, Gloria asked me if I could put a band together for the tenth anniversary of the charity. These events invariably feature an auction and on this occasion the auctioneer was Lord Archer, the famous politician, author and ex-convict.

'Hands up all the men over 50!' he ordered, as his opening line.

We dutifully obeyed.

'How many have NOT had your PSA levels checked?' he growled.

Most of us kept our hands up.

'Well do it this week,' he roared.

My dear friend Ian Wallace, who played drums for so many famous names, had warned us all before he died from prostate cancer, 'Get yourselves checked out before it's too late.' And of course, true to form, I did absolutely nothing. Another old pal, drummer Kenney Jones, asked me to join him in a charity event – a concert at Hurtwood Park Polo Club for his prostate cancer charity. I later discovered Kenney was already undergoing treatment for the disease. Happily, he has made an excellent recovery. But despite all the omens, I still didn't get myself checked out.

But this time, I just couldn't ignore a lord of the realm and so I had a blood test to determine my PSA level. Prostate-specific antigen (PSA) is a substance produced by the prostate gland and elevated levels may indicate prostate cancer. I was just in time. Thanks Jeffrey. I like him despite his murky past – because that night he saved my life. I have since become involved in charity work for Prostate Cancer UK. I also recorded a version of 'Give Peace a Chance' for the British Red Cross. We are now in our fourth year of me leading a band and my pals Rod and Penny, plus Roger Taylor, Steve Harley, Kenney Jones, Sam Tanner, Ben Mills, Pat Davey and Harry James have regularly helped in supporting the cause.

One of my fondest memories in regard to charity events was the Music for UNICEF (The United Nations Children's Fund) Concert in 1979, featuring some very big names, who donated their performance royalties and those from one song each to UNICEF. Among others, there were performances from Abba, the Bee Gees, Donna Summer, Olivia Newton-John, Elton, Rod, Rita Coolidge and Kris Kristofferson, who sang 'Tonight's the Night'. I had to try and get him to sing harmony with Rod – something he was quite unused to! He was fun, and happy to be involved as we all were.

The filmed concert took place at the United Nations General Assembly in New York and getting to run around such a famous room was quite something. It was the same venue where, in 1960, Soviet leader Nikita Khrushchev famously banged his shoe on his delegate desk, shouting 'Nyet! Nyet!' in protest at a speech delegate from the Philippines. Of course, the first thing I did when I got into the room was to pound a podium and shout in my best Russian, 'Nyet! Nyet!' Unfortunately, my actions didn't resonate quite so much among the assembled throng, but I think it was because I was wearing sneakers.

The whole vibe was magical. Everyone was in and out of each other's dressing rooms, and Henry Winkler, aka the Fonz, turned out to be a lovely man. He introduced our band and hung out with us the whole day. It always amazes me how intrigued other people – particularly actors – are with what we do. I continue to be surprised at the interest and attraction that old rockers create.

The United Nations building was such an unusual venue to do a show with an audience, and at the end of the concert all the performers took to the stage, before we were lauded with a reception, hosted by Kurt Waldheim, the Secretary General of the UN.

The event raised a huge amount of money, which is more than can be said at my attempt to raise some funds some fifteen years later following the Northridge earthquake. Jane and I were living in Laurel Canyon and Camille was just 3 years old. On 17 January 1994, we were woken in the middle of the night to the sound of broken glass as an entire collection of Waterford crystal leaped from the shelves and smashed on the floor. The whole house was shaking violently. I ran and got Camille and we huddled together in the arch of the doorway to our bedroom. I was nervous, but also fascinated as the whole experience was bizarre and surreal. There was a huge bang as the power line transformers exploded outside the house. Then the lights went out. Now, I was more than nervous. I feared sparks from power lines might ignite the gas from the ruptured pipes.

I grabbed my shoes and a flashlight from the bedside table and once the first shock was over, I went outside to check on my neighbours. There was glass everywhere, but no real damage to the property. We took in a young woman who was on her own and very anxious. Tim Noyes, our neighbour on the other side, was a Vietnam vet and ex-helicopter pilot. An all-round fantastic guy, whose military training kicked in and who reassured us. We checked that the gas wasn't leaking and then sat around awaiting the dawn, while listening on the radio to reports of freeways collapsing and major structural damage throughout the city. I was surprised by my own reaction as I actually remained reasonably calm, although I did experience a momentary religious conversion, pleading with God not to let us die. It was strange that the previous evening Jane had an intuition that something was going to happen and had wanted Camille to sleep in our bed.

The city was in chaos. Freeways had caved in, apartment complexes had collapsed, thousands of buildings had to be demolished and when the extent of the disaster was eventually made public, the death toll had reached over sixty, with nearly 9,000 injured. Damage to property and infrastructure was estimated to be approaching $50 billion.

Jane and I felt that we had to do something to help. I was due to take a six-week break from the *Unplugged* tour, but a holiday in these circumstances seemed somehow facile. Taking our initiative from Midge Ure, who co-organised *Band Aid* and *Live Aid* with Bob Geldof, we decided to try and put on a concert to raise some money for those affected. I called my old friend and Rod's previous road manager, Pete Buckland, who, in very little time, had arranged all the infrastructure including the Universal Amphitheatre as a venue, American Airlines, trucking companies, PA, lights, publicist, and a television company to film the event. I discovered that everyone wanted to help – except the artists.

I thought that if a child of Irish immigrants living in LA was prepared to sacrifice his time to bring this together, then local bands like Guns 'N' Roses and Van Halen would have supported their local people. I started calling people to ask if they would do a free concert. Through various contacts I got hold of Don Henley of the Eagles who was very hot at the time. He very generously agreed to perform, and I thought that would start the ball rolling, but I was wrong. I rang Tom Petty's manager, whose response was, 'Just 'cos you got Don Henley, well that cuts no ice. Tom Petty is a much bigger name.'

Meanwhile we discovered that a guy called Jeff Wald was trying to arrange a similar event. He managed Helen Reddy, Donna Summer, David Crosby and Sly Stallone. So, not wanting to duplicate the event, we joined forces, which at the time seemed sensible. But it wasn't. I hadn't realised Wald's difficult reputation was widespread. Hot tempered and fond of a punch-up, he had already alienated many musicians and he couldn't persuade anyone to contribute. I now had a new respect for Bob Geldof and Midge. Several musicians claimed they were going to do their own thing, but never did.

To the shame of the artistic community in LA, following such a disaster in their home town, there were no major fund-raising concerts. I also experienced a negative effect from several charities who, thinking at the outset that this was going to be a big deal, wanted a part of the action. I'd already decided that any monies we made would be donated to the Red Cross and another local charity. I came under pressure from organisations who were pressurising me to change my mind about the intended recipients.

Their 'hard sell' really disappointed me – the charities didn't seem to be interested in what they could do for the newly homeless victims, but more about raising their profile. I was left feeling very dispirited and disappointed in some of my fellow human beings. No good deed goes unpunished.

★★★

On the club circuit there is a gentleman named Bevo, who has a PA company that he has owned for years. He is also a great sound mixer, so you know you're in good hands when you arrive at the club and Bevo greets you. We are all very fond of Bevo, but he might be described as a bit of a rough diamond.

For reasons best known to nobody, he was once asked to supply a sound system for a disco for some young royals and a deal was made to rent his kit from 6 p.m. until midnight. He showed up at the palace, installed the PA and retired outside for a snooze in his van.

At about 11.30 p.m. he wandered in to the disco to see assorted royals throwing themselves round the room. In the privacy of their own home they certainly know how to party. Mad abandon doesn't begin to describe it. At around midnight, Bevo signalled to the DJ by tapping his watch that there should be a winding down of the revelry. The DJ suggested another fifteen minutes or so and Bevo reluctantly agreed. He still had to pack up the gear and wanted to go home to bed. One gets the feeling that Bevo couldn't care less about being in the company of the future monarch.

By 12.30 a.m. it became clear no one wanted to stop, so Bevo wandered over to the wall plug and simply pulled it out. In a freeze frame moment, everyone was caught out. You know that thing when you're having to yell a conversation with someone in a club or bar and it suddenly goes quiet. Hundreds of pairs of eyes swivelled towards Bevo, but he couldn't care less.

'I was only booked till midnight,' he announced, slightly defensively, but determined to hold his ground. A chorus of aristocratic disapproval was unleashed.

'What do you think you're doing?'

'We are just warming up.'

'It's not time for the carriages yet!'

'What a nerve! It's still early.'

'I say, you can't do this!'

'Oh yes I can. Just watch me.' Devo was unimpressed and began to unplug some of the cables.

'Can't we work something out?' suggested a young prince.

Bevo paused. 'What did you have in mind?'

'How about another £500 for a couple of hours?'

'OK.' Bevo agreed and the party took off once more. As the 2.30 a.m. deadline approached, a small altercation began as Bevo was surrounded by various guests, insisting that the party continue. Foolishly, from behind, one of them put his hand roughly on Bevo's shoulder. In one swift movement our hero grabbed the arm, pivoted quickly to one side and using his hip, threw his would-be assailant to the floor.

Shock! Horror! The audience gasped as they looked down on this elegant man in a tuxedo, recovering himself. Just as Bevo was led away by security he was heard to say, 'How was I to know he was the fuckin' King of Tonga?'

I mention Bevo because he worked with the band, initially called Apart from Rod, that I formed in 2011. It was really the brainchild of my old friend, guitarist Gary Grainger. I had jammed at a big festival with the Jones Gang (Kenney's outfit) and got on very well with ex-Bad Company singer Robert Hart. So, Gary and I asked him if he wanted to start a new band.

That turned out to be a momentous stroke of luck because he introduced us to what was to become the core of Jim Cregan & Co. Along with Gary and Robert, we auditioned Pat Davey on bass, drummer Harry James and Sam Tanner on keyboards. Eight bars into the first tune I knew I had struck gold. What a rhythm section! Pat, Sam and Harry are a force of nature. They compare with some of the best in the world and if you check my résumé, you will see I've played with some very fine players. They are now my dearest friends and when we play together there's still that warmth and fun that we stumbled upon on day one.

Robert Hart then received an offer he couldn't refuse and joined Manfred Mann's Earth Band. After a couple of false starts we found Ben Mills, another great vocalist and excellent on guitar and keys. He fitted right in from the beginning which reminds me to mention that your personality and attitude are equally important if you want to work in this business. Sadly, Gary had to drop out because of illness, from which he is happily recovering, but I miss him. We were lucky enough to have Robin Le Mesurier step in for a while, but it was hard for him to stay in the band as the commute from Los Angeles was a bit inconvenient! We were managed for a while by Thunder singer Danny Bowes who suggested we drop the Apart from Rod band name and call ourselves Cregan & Co. It must have been a good idea, because we still perform regularly around the country. Thanks Danny!

I reunited with Roger Chapman in 2005 for live performances and then a solo album *One More Time For Peace* a couple of years later. Bob Dylan's album, *Modern Times*, was the influence that led us in that direction. Of course, I love acoustic music and had made some recordings with Rod at my home studio that Roger liked. We did a lot of pre-production at my house, but the record itself was recorded quite quickly because we had the right players. It's a bit like casting a movie: if the chemistry is good, you don't have to work very hard. I used an old trick from my Farm Dog days of having two guitarists playing together. The rapport brings an extra dimension, as they play off each other. Also, there's safety in numbers. People often play their best if the track is being recorded live, as opposed to everyone overdubbing individually to a click or drum loop.

I see no need to stop doing something I love. I enjoy all the aspects of it, writing being my favourite but also producing and performing on stage. Who knows what else the future will bring … all the usual stuff: write a song, produce a record, write a book, play a gig and stay out of jail.

At a small family gathering, some years ago, my nephew James Samson introduced me to his friend David Hole. David's son was then a 15-year-old songwriter named Charlie and, as fathers do worldwide, David told me that his son was pretty amazing and pressed a CD into my hand. This sort of thing happens to me with some regularity and I've only once before thought the artist was any good. But I listened to the CD and quickly realised that Charlie Hole was a helluva singer and lyricist. A tiny moment of trumpeting. Having written with some great lyricists over the years, I think I'm an excellent judge … and Charlie is that good.

Pause for a story: at the prestigious Ivor Novello Awards ceremony, lyricist Barry Mason is being honoured for writing the lyric for 'Delilah', the hit for Tom Jones. As Barry is about to exit the men's room, a man enters, whistling the song.

'I wrote that,' Barry smiles at the man.

The guy paused and looked him up and down.

'No, that was written by Les Reed and you're not Les Reed.'

'Ahh yes, but I wrote the lyric to Les's music.'

'Yeah, but I wasn't whistling the bloody lyric, was I?'

Anyway, I invited Charlie to my house in Surrey to record a song to see if it was going to work out. It worked out great. I called my old friend Robert Allan, who is a very successful publishing lawyer in London, to ask him if he'd like to manage Charlie with me. And the adventure began. Robert set up a meeting with Lance Freed, the legendary music publisher in LA, and I play him just one song called 'Spark'. Lance listened in rapt attention and when the music stopped, said, 'I'll sign him, but he has to finish school first.' Fair enough, I thought.

Since then, Charlie and I have recorded two albums, a couple of EPs and a single or two and we have a record deal. It's a co-venture with my label Cocomack records. Charlie will be one of those artists that once he gets a break, the fans will also discover what I found in him. Charlie also understands the 10,000 hours concept and he plays all the time in order to reach that amount of 'deliberate practice'. Overnight success is often followed by overnight downfall.

My latest venture is a result of the endeavours and spirit of an indomitable woman. Anne Dunsmore is a force of nature. She has the most energy of anyone I know. A long-time political fundraiser for US presidents, she knows people from all walks of life. About ten years ago she befriended my California family during a time of crisis and was hugely instrumental in resolving some difficult issues.

Fast forward to summer 2018, Anne is in London and comes to see Cregan & Co. play a gig.

'I'm blown away! You guys are great.' She then went on to explain that she had set up a non-profit organisation, Angel Force USA, to help US veterans with PTSD and other difficulties. She told me that as many as twenty 'vets' were committing suicide *every day* – a figure that I found to be extraordinary. Anne said she wanted to bring us to California to be part of the charity and help raise funds. To be honest, I thought the chances of her getting this done were next to zero. But it was such a worthy cause we all agreed. At Anne's invitation my old pal Neil Byford and I went to California and I wrote a song, 'The One That Got Away', with her musician friends, a band called the Side Deal. We wrote the music one day, the lyric the next and went into the studio and recorded it on the third. Almost biblical … it's quite upbeat and tender but it has a subtext that touches on the possibility of saving someone from suicide. On 1 December 2018, Cregan & Co. and the Side Deal played a charity fundraiser in a ballroom in Newport Beach, California. The event raised $200,000. A pretty good start. Anne is suggesting we take this idea and repeat it in other cities and eventually internationally. This time I'm not doubting that she can do it. I know she will.

Despite parting company professionally in 1994, Rod and I have remained best friends. For about twenty years he suffered from writer's block to the extent that I had practically given up on explaining it could still be fun and rewarding to create new music. Then, sometime in 2012, I'm invited to Sunday dinner at his postcode in Essex. 'Why don't you come a bit earlier and bring a guitar,' he says. My response was direct, 'OK that's easy.'

I break out my Martin twelve string and we sit in the living room and I start to play a few cowboy chords. Those are the ones at the bottom of the neck that any beginner learns. A bit of melody as it comes to me and we're off. Rod picks up the tune and moves it on to a place that works for him. The chorus just falls out of the sky and into our laps. We tweak it a bit and within about an hour or two we have the bulk of the song. I've been recording each new development on my iPhone.

The next day, after a night of roast dinner and fine wine, we re-visit the work and realise it could do with a bridge or middle eight. That too takes no time at all.

'I'll knock up a rough track at home and send it to you in a day or two,' I say as I get ready to drive away.

It was only when I started work on it that I recognised it was already pretty good.

I took the rough work tape from my iPhone and dumped it into 'Pro Tools'.

By manipulating it in the computer and adding new instruments I could give the song a better sound. I sent the new version over and Rod replied that he loved it and it was to be called 'Brighton Beach'. We had restarted his songwriting and happily, he's gone on to finish three albums. Good work ...

I was very happily surprised and honoured when Rod and Penny asked me to be best man at their wedding. I had watched with interest how their romance had developed. Penny would come and hang with Robin, Jules and me quite often if she was feeling a little insecure about how things were going. We always encouraged her, for even if Rod was taking his time about proposing, we were all convinced she was absolutely the right woman for him. The ceremony took place in an old monastery in the Italian Riviera near Portofino in June 2007. Sitting high up on a bluff, we looked out with spectacular views over the Mediterranean. There were many varied events from a string quartet to waiters singing opera, bagpipers and a great rock band that I jammed with into the early hours. I was also the MC and it fell to me to announce the couple as they entered the dining area.

'Ladies and gentlemen, please be upstanding. It gives me great pleasure to welcome for the very first time, Mr & Mrs Roderick David Esmeralda Tinkerbell Mildred Theodora Stewart.'

Well somebody had to.

I couldn't be happier that Rod is godfather to my youngest child, Ava. Ava brings so much laughter and joy into our home and has developed a wicked sense of humour. Artistic and a psycho-gymnast, she would happily cartwheel anywhere rather than walk. After joining the local Sea Scouts, she has developed all sorts of wonderful skills. She sails and paddleboards on the river outside our home. She can easily burn the house down using sparks made from a flint and steel while serenading you with her ukulele. She is an excellent student, coming top in her year group. She wants to go to Oxford University and I believe she will do it. She is loved without reservation.

Camille is now a successful model and actor. She is married and lives in LA with her delightful and altogether-too-good-looking husband, William Overby. She has appeared in several movies and TV shows, dozens of high-profile commercials and numerous print campaigns. She is about to follow in her mother's footsteps by designing a line of women's fashion wear. Camille has an unerring eye for style and effortlessly surrounds herself with examples of exquisite taste. My first-born child, she radiates goodness and continually charms us with her beauty, wit and graciousness. With Camille you really can know 'True Love'. She is already becoming the matriarch of this branch of the family. Unflappable and resourceful, just ask her, 'Can you make dinner for twenty people?'

'No problem.' What a woman!

Mack is 22 years old and has the soul of a Texas bluesman from the 1950s. I tried my best to talk him out of it … but he was always going to form a band. And he couldn't wait. Neither could I, at his age. He is an amazingly elegant and soulful player, a writer, a singer and a mesmerising front man. So, watch out. He gives me chills when he opens up on that guitar. Loads better than me; 'the student eclipses the teacher.' We are forever connected through music and I'm never happier than when we just jam around the house. Mack is now studying for his degree at Paul McCartney's Liverpool Institute of Performing Arts (LIPA), so he comes and stays with me regularly. This is a huge bonus. I love him so much. How fortunate am I to be really close to all my children?

Looking back over my career, I have much to be thankful for. I once remarked to my dad, 'I just want to do this for a year. See how it goes.' That was over fifty years ago and I'm still seeing how it goes. It goes quite well, I suppose. But do I see myself as a success? There's been something rattling around in what's left of my brain regarding exactly that.

All that time in Los Angeles I was always under the impression that success was how much stuff you had. The absolute minimum was a great house with a pool in a swanky area. A beautiful partner, fabulous kids in the best schools, several cool cars and a job that people admired and/or envied. If you had all this, you had to be happy. You'd made it or were on your way.

There was no escaping this point of view. It was all that mattered. I remember people worrying about having the wrong table when eating lunch at Morton's Beverly Hills' restaurant or not being invited to Swifty Lazar's post-Oscar party.

Of course, this generalisation is somewhat unfair. But to quote actor Carrie Fisher in her book *Surrender the Pink*, 'We don't need real friends here in LA because we do fake friends so well.' Sadly, this resonated deeply with me, despite the fact that I still have some true friends there.

Although Mandy and I had split up, we live close to each other, so that Ava has the stability of two doting parents. I had been forever trying to persuade Mandy to move to Christchurch in Dorset, as my close and extended family lived there. I wanted Ava to grow up around her cousins and to live near the sea and be able to share my love of sailing. This had been a big part of my childhood and I hoped it could be Ava's too. It wasn't Mandy's first choice to be away from easy access to London, but she could see that it was a beautiful gift for Ava. She, very generously, agreed to the move and we found separate houses in the town.

But to make my point about success, I have now lived by the river for several years and I am beginning to feel successful at last. I don't need much. I'm close to my birth family, all of them within walking distance. I have a tiny boat named *Love Me Tender*. I can gently motor down through the beautiful natural harbour to a pristine beach where the family have beach huts, offering rustic sleepovers with stunning views of sunsets and shining dawns. It's peaceful. There's not much edge. Sure, there's a pecking order here too but nobody really cares. We are hard to impress. You may have lots of stuff, but you better be a nice guy too or it's meaningless.

I still play music. I still write songs. I still produce records and no matter what car I drive or where I live, at long last, I know what success is.

It's something you carry in your heart. It's the capacity to find contentment in small pleasures. Like the joy in raising your kids or caring for a friend, and above all sharing love wherever you can.

Forever.

Index